The ESSENTIALS® of

REGISTERED TRADEMARK

UNITED STATES HISTORY

1841 to 1877
Westward Expansion
and the Civil War

Steven E. Woodworth, Ph.D.

Assistant Professor of History
Toccoa Falls College
Toccoa, Georgia

Research and Education Association
61 Ethel Road West
Piscataway, New Jersey 08854

THE ESSENTIALS ®
OF UNITED STATES HISTORY
1841 to 1877
Westward Expansion and the Civil War

Printed in the United States of America

Library of Congress Catalog Card Number 89-62464

International Standard Book Number 0-87891-714-4

REVISED PRINTING, 1992

ESSENTIALS is a registered trademark of
Research and Education Association, Piscataway, New Jersey 08854

What the "Essentials of History" Will Do for You

REA's "Essentials of History" series offers a new approach to the study of history that is different from what has been available previously. Each book in the series has been designed to steer a sensible middle course, by including neither too much nor too little information.

Compared with conventional history outlines, the "Essentials of History" offer far more detail, with fuller explanations and interpretations of historical events and developments. Compared with voluminous historical tomes and textbooks, the "Essentials of History" offer a far more concise, less ponderous overview of each of the periods they cover.

The "Essentials of History" are intended primarily to aid students in studying history, doing homework, writing papers and preparing for exams. The books are organized to provide quick access to information and explanations of the important events, dates, and persons of the period. The books can be used in conjunction with any text. They will save hours of study and preparation time while providing a firm grasp and insightful understanding of the subject matter.

Instructors too will find the "Essentials of History" useful. The books can assist in reviewing or modifying course outlines. They also can assist with preparation of exams, as well as serve as an efficient memory refresher.

In sum, the "Essentials of History" will prove to be handy reference sources at all times.

The authors of the series are respected experts in their fields. They present clear, well-reasoned explanations and interpretations of the complex political, social, cultural, economic and philosophical issues and developments which characterize each era.

In preparing these books REA has made every effort to assure their accuracy and maximum usefulness. We are confident that each book will prove enjoyable and valuable to its user.

Dr. Max Fogiel, Program Director

About the Author

Steven E. Woodworth received the Rice Presidential Recognition Award in 1983, a scholarship from the University of Hamburg German Academic Exchange Service in 1982-1983, and a Rice University Graduate Fellowship from 1983 to 1987. His professional memberships include the American Historical Association, the Southern Historical Association, and the Conference on Faith and History. His special expertise includes the Civil War and Reconstruction era, the U.S. Constitution and legal history, U.S. military history, and U.S. colonial and revolutionary history. He is the author of *Jefferson Davis and His Generals: The Failure of Confederate Command in the West.*

Dr. Woodworth is currently an assistant professor of History at Toccoa Falls College in Toccoa, Georgia. He was previously an instructor at Bartlesville Wesleyan College in Bartlesville, Oklahoma.

CONTENTS

CHAPTER 1

TYLER, POLK, AND THE WESTWARD EXPANSION

1.1 TYLER AND THE WHIGS

When William Henry Harrison became president, he immediately began to rely on Whig leader Henry Clay for advice and direction, just as Clay had planned and expected he would. He appointed to his cabinet those whom Clay suggested, and at Clay's behest he called a special session of Congress to vote the Whig legislative program into action. To the Whigs' dismay, Harrison died of pneumonia just one month into his term, to be replaced by Vice President John Tyler.

A states'-rights southerner and a strict constitutionalist who had been placed on the Whig ticket to draw southern votes, Tyler rejected the entire Whig program of a national bank, high protective tariffs, and federally funded internal improvements (roads, canals, etc.). Clay stubbornly determined to push the program through anyway. In the resulting legislative confrontations, Tyler vetoed a number of Whig-sponsored bills.

The Whigs were furious. Every cabinet member but one

resigned in protest. Tyler was officially expelled from the party and made the target of the first serious impeachment attempt. (It failed.) In opposition to Tyler over the next few years the Whigs, under the leadership of Clay, transformed themselves from a loose grouping of diverse factions to a coherent political party with an elaborate organization.

One piece of important legislation that did get passed during Tyler's administration was the Preemption Act (1841), allowing settlers who had squatted on unsurveyed federal lands first chance to buy the land (up to 160 acres at low prices) once it was put on the market.

1.2   THE WEBSTER-ASHBURTON TREATY

The member of Tyler's cabinet who did not immediately resign in protest was Secretary of State Daniel Webster. He stayed on to negotiate the Webster-Ashburton Treaty with Great Britain.

There were at this time several causes of tension between the U.S. and Great Britain:

1) The Canada-Maine boundary in the area of the Aroostook Valley was disputed. British efforts to build a military road through the disputed area led to reaction by Maine militia in a bloodless confrontation known as the "Aroostook War" (1838).

2) The *Caroline* Affair (1837) involved an American ship, the *Caroline*, that had been carrying supplies to Canadian rebels. It was burned by Canadian loyalists who crossed the U.S. border in order to do so.

3) In the *Creole* Incident, Britain declined to return es-

caped slaves who had taken over a U.S. merchant ship, the *Creole*, and sailed to the British-owned Bahamas.

4) British naval vessels, patrolling the African coast to suppress slave-smuggling, sometimes stopped and searched American ships.

The Webster-Ashburton Treaty (1842) dealt with these problems in a spirit of mutual concession and forebearance:

1) Conflicting claims along the Canada-Maine boundary were compromised.

2) The British expressed regret for the destruction of the *Caroline*.

3) The British promised to avoid "officious interference" in freeing slaves in cases such as that of the *Creole*.

4) Both countries agreed to cooperate in patrolling the African coast to prevent slave-smuggling.

The Webster-Ashburton Treaty was also important in that it helped create an atmosphere of compromise and forebearance in U.S.-British relations.

After negotiating the treaty, Webster too resigned from Tyler's cabinet.

1.3   THE TEXAS ISSUE

Rejected by the Whigs and without ties to the Democrats, Tyler was a politician without a party but not without ambitions. Hoping to gather a political following of his own, he sought an issue with powerful appeal and believed he had found it in the question of Texas annexation.

The Republic of Texas had gained its independence from Mexico in 1836 and, since most of its settlers had come from the U.S., immediately sought admission as a state. It was rejected because anti-slavery forces in Congress resented the presence of slavery in Texas and because Mexico threatened war should the U.S. annex Texas.

To excite American jealousy and thus hasten annexation, Texas President Sam Houston made much show of negotiating for closer relations with Great Britain. Southerners feared that Britain, which opposed slavery, might bring about its abolition in Texas and then use Texas as a base from which to undermine slavery in the American South. Other Americans were disturbed at the possibility of a British presence in Texas because of the obstacle it would present to what many Americans were coming to believe – and what New York journalist John L. O'Sullivan would soon express – as America's "manifest destiny to overspread the continent."

Tyler's new secretary of state, John C. Calhoun, negotiated an annexation treaty with Texas. Calhoun's identification with extreme pro-slavery forces and his insertion in the treaty of pro-slavery statements brought the treaty's rejection by the Senate (1844). Nevertheless the Texas issue had been injected into national politics and could not be made to go away.

1.4   THE ELECTION OF 1844

Democratic front-runner Martin Van Buren and Whig front-runner Henry Clay agreed privately that neither would endorse Texas annexation and that it would not become a campaign issue, but expansionists at the Democratic convention succeeded in dumping Van Buren in favor of James K. Polk. Polk, called

"Young Hickory" by his supporters, was a staunch Jacksonian who opposed protective tariffs and a national bank but, most important, favored territorial expansion, including not only annexation of Texas but also occupation of all the Oregon country (up to latitude 54° 40') hitherto jointly occupied by the U.S. and Britain. The latter claim was expressed in his campaign slogan, "Fifty-four forty or fight."

Tyler, despite his introduction of the issue that was to decide that year's presidential campaign, was unable to build a party of his own and withdrew from the race.

The Whigs nominated Clay, who continued to oppose Texas annexation but, sensing the mood of the country was against him, began to equivocate. His wavering cost him votes among those northerners who were extremely sensitive to the issue of slavery and believed that the settlement, independence, and proposed annexation of Texas was a gigantic plot to add slave states to the Union. Some of these voters shifted to the Liberty party.

The anti-slavery Liberty party nominated James G. Birney. Apparently because of Clay's wavering on the Texas issue, Birney was able to take enough votes away from Clay in New York to give that state, and thus the election, to Polk.

Tyler, as a lame-duck President, made one more attempt to achieve Texas annexation before leaving office. By means of a joint resolution, which unlike a treaty required only a simple majority rather than a two-thirds vote, he was successful in getting the measure through Congress. Texas was finally admitted to the Union (1845).

1.5   POLK AS PRESIDENT

Though a relatively unknown "dark horse" at the time of his nomination for the Presidency, Polk had considerable political experience within his home state of Tennessee and was an adept politician. He turned out to be a skillful and effective President.

As a good Jacksonian, Polk favored a low, revenue-only tariff rather than a high, protective tariff. This he obtained in the Walker Tariff (1846). He also opposed a national debt and a national bank and re-established Van Buren's Independent Sub-Treasury system, which then remained in effect until 1920.

1.6   THE SETTLEMENT OF OREGON

A major issue in the election campaign of 1844, Oregon at this time comprised all the land bounded on the east by the Rockies, the west by the Pacific, the south by latitude 42°, and the north by the boundary of Russian-held Alaska at 54° 40'. Oregon had been visited by Lewis and Clark and in later years by American fur traders and especially missionaries such as Jason Lee and Marcus Whitman. Their reports sparked interest in Oregon's favorable soil and climate. During the first half of the 1840s, some 6000 Americans had taken the 2000-mile, six-month journey on the Oregon Trail, from Independence, Missouri, across the plains along the Platte River, through the Rockies at South Pass, and down the Snake River to their new homesteads. Most of them settled in the Willamette Valley, south of the Columbia River.

The area had been under the joint occupation of the U.S. and Great Britain since 1818, but Democrats in the election of 1844 had called for U.S. ownership of all of Oregon. Though this stand had helped him win the election, Polk had little de-

THE OREGON TREATY

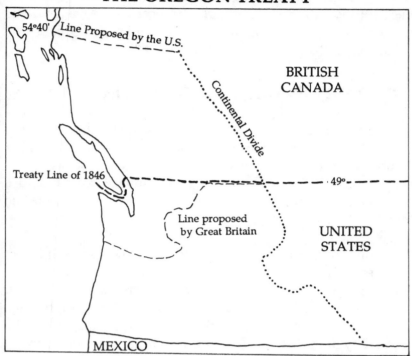

sire to fight the British for land he considered unsuitable for agriculture and unavailable for slavery, which he favored. This was all the more so since trouble seemed to be brewing with Mexico over territory Polk considered far more desirable (See Section 1.8).

The British, for their part, hoped to obtain the area north of the Columbia River, including the natural harbor of Puget Sound (one of only three on the Pacific coast), with its adjoining Strait of Juan de Fuca.

By the terms of the Oregon Treaty (1846), a compromise solution was reached. The current U.S.-Canada boundary east of the Rockies (49°) was extended westward to the Pacific, thus securing Puget Sound and shared use of the Strait of Juan de Fuca for the U.S. Some northern Democrats were angered and felt betrayed by Polk's failure to insist on all of Oregon, but the Senate readily accepted the treaty.

1.7   THE MORMON MIGRATION

Aside from the thousands of Americans who streamed west on the Oregon Trail during the early 1840s and the smaller number who migrated to what was then Mexican-held California, another large group of Americans moved west but to a different destination and for different reasons. These were the Mormons.

Members of a unique religion founded by Joseph Smith at Palmyra, New York in the 1820s, Mormons, often in trouble with their neighbors, had been forced to migrate to Kirtland, Ohio; Clay County, Missouri; and finally, Nauvoo, Illinois. There, on the banks of the Mississippi River, they built the largest city in the state, had their own militia, and were a political force to be reckoned with.

In 1844 Mormon dissidents published a newspaper critical of church leader Smith and his newly announced doctrine of polygamy. Smith had their printing press destroyed. Arrested by Illinois authorities, Smith and his brother were confined to a jail in Carthage, Illinois, but later killed by a crowd of hostile non-Mormons who forced their way into the jail.

The Mormons then decided to migrate to the Far West, preferably someplace outside U.S. jurisdiction. Their decision to leave was hastened by pressure from their non-Mormon neighbors, among whom anti-Mormon feeling ran high as a response to polygamy and the Mormons' monolithic social and political structure.

WESTERN TRAILS IN THE 1840s

Under the leadership of new church leader Brigham Young some 85,000 Mormons trekked overland in 1846 to settle near the Great Salt Lake in what is now Utah (but was then owned by Mexico). Young founded the Mormon republic of Deseret and openly preached (and practiced) polygamy.

After Deseret's annexation by the U.S. as part of the Mexican Cession (see Section 1.9), Young was made territorial governor of Utah. Nevertheless, friction developed with the federal government. By 1857 public outrage over polygamy prompted then President James Buchanan to replace Young with a non-Mormon governor. Threats of Mormon defiance led Buchanan to send 2500 army troops to compel Mormon obedience to federal law. Young responded by calling out the Mormon militia and blocking the passes through which the army would have to advance. This standoff, known as the "Mormon War," was resolved in 1858, with the Mormons accepting the new governor and Buchanan issuing a general pardon.

1.8   THE COMING OF WAR WITH MEXICO

For some time American interest had been growing in the far western lands then held by Mexico:

1) Since the 1820s Americans had been trading with Santa Fe and other Mexican settlements along the Rio Grande by means of the Santa Fe Trail. Though not extensive enough to be of economic importance the trade aroused further American interest in the area.

2) Also, since the 1820s, American "mountain men," trappers who sought beaver pelts in the streams of the Rockies, had explored the mountains of the Far West, opening new trails and discovering fertile lands. They later served as guides for settlers moving west.

3) At the same time whaling ships and other American vessels had carried on a thriving trade with the Mexican settlements on the coast of California.

4) Beginning in 1841, American settlers came overland to California by means of the California Trail, a branch from the Oregon Trail that turned southwest in the Rockies and crossed Nevada along the Humbolt River. By 1846 several hundred Americans lived in California.

The steady flow of American pioneers into Mexican-held areas of the Far West led to conflicting territorial desires and was thus an underlying cause of the Mexican War. Several more immediate causes existed:

1) Mexico's ineffective government was unable to protect the lives and property of American citizens in Mexico during the country's frequent and recurring revolutions and repeatedly declined to pay American claims for damages even when such claims were supported by the findings of mutually agreed upon arbitration.

2) Mexico had not reconciled itself to the loss of Texas and considered its annexation by the U.S. a hostile act.

3) The southern boundary of Texas was disputed. Whereas first the independent Republic of Texas and now the U.S. claimed the Rio Grande as the boundary, Mexico claimed the Nueces River, 130 miles farther north, because it had been the boundary of the province of Texas when it had been part of Mexico.

4) Mexican suspicions had been aroused regarding U.S. designs on California when, in 1842, a U.S. naval force under Commodore Thomas Catsby Jones had seized the province in the mistaken belief that war had broken out between the U.S. and Mexico. When the mistake was discovered, the province was returned and apologies made.

5) Mexican politicians had so inflamed the Mexican people against the U.S. that no Mexican leader could afford to take the risk of appearing to make concessions to the U.S. for fear of being overthrown.

Though Mexico broke diplomatic relations with the U.S. immediately upon Texas' admission to the Union, there still seemed to be some hope of a peaceful settlement. In the fall of 1845 Polk sent John Slidell to Mexico City with a proposal for a peaceful settlement of the differences between the two countries. Slidell was empowered to cancel the damage claims and pay $5,000,000 for the disputed land in southern Texas. He was also authorized to offer $25,000,000 for California and $5,000,000 for other Mexican territory in the Far West. Polk was especially anxious to obtain California because he feared the British would snatch it from Mexico's extremely weak grasp.

Nothing came of these attempts at negotiation. Racked by coup and countercoup, the Mexican government refused even to receive Slidell.

Polk thereupon sent U.S. troops into the disputed territory in southern Texas. A force under General Zachary Taylor (who was nicknamed "Old Rough and Ready") took up a position just north of the Rio Grande. Eight days later, April 5, 1846, Mexican troops attacked an American patrol. When news of the clash reached Washington, Polk sought and received from Congress a declaration of war against Mexico, May 13, 1846.

1.9   THE MEXICAN WAR

Americans were sharply divided about the war. Some favored it because they felt Mexico had provoked the war or because they felt it was the destiny of America to spread the blessings of freedom to oppressed peoples. Others opposed the war. Some, primarily Polk's political enemies the Whigs, accused the President of having provoked it. Others, generally northern abolitionists, saw in the war the work of a vast conspiracy of southern slaveholders greedy for more slave territory.

In planning military strategy, Polk showed genuine skill. American strategy consisted originally of a three-pronged attack:

1) a land movement westward through New Mexico into California,

2) a sea movement against California, and

3) a land movement southward into Mexico.

The first prong of this three-pronged strategy, the advance through New Mexico and into California, was led by Colonel Stephen W. Kearny. Kearny's force easily secured New Mexico, entering Santa Fe August 16, 1846, before continuing west to California. There American settlers, aided by an Army exploring party under John C. Frémont, had already revolted against Mexico's weak rule in what was called the Bear Flag Revolt.

As part of the second prong of U.S. strategy, naval forces under Commodore John D. Sloat had seized Monterey and declared California to be part of the United States. Forces put ashore by Commodore Robert Stockton joined with Kearny's troops to defeat the Mexicans at the Battle of San Gabriel, January 1847, and complete the conquest of California.

The third prong of the American strategy, an advance southward into Mexico, was itself divided into two parts:

1) Troops under Colonel Alexander W. Doniphan defeated Mexicans at El Brazito (December 25-28, 1846) to take El Paso, and then proceeded southward, winning the Battle of Sacramento (February 28, 1847) to take the city of Chihuahua, capital of the Mexican province of that name.

2) The main southward thrust, however, was made by a

much larger American army under General Zachary Taylor. After badly defeating larger Mexican forces at the battles of Palo Alto (May 7, 1846) and Resaca de la Palma (May 8, 1846), Taylor advanced into Mexico and defeated an even larger Mexican force at the Battle of Monterey (September 20-24, 1846). Then, after substantial numbers of his troops had been transferred to other sectors of the war, he successfully withstood, though badly outnumbered, an attack by a Mexican force under Antonia Lopez de Santa Anna at the Battle of Buena Vista, February 22-23, 1847.

Despite the success of all three parts of the American strategy, the Mexicans refused to negotiate. Polk therefore ordered U.S. forces under General Winfield Scott to land on the east coast of Mexico, march inland, and take Mexico City.

Scott landed at Veracruz March 9, 1847, and by March 27 had captured the city with the loss of only twenty American lives. He advanced from there, being careful to maintain good discipline and avoid atrocities in the countryside. At Cerro Gord (April 18, 1847), in what has been called "the most important single battle of the war," Scott outflanked and soundly defeated a superior enemy force in a seemingly impregnable position. After beating another Mexican army at Churubusco (August 19-20, 1847), Scott paused outside Mexico City to offer the Mexicans another chance to negotiate. When they declined, U.S. forces stormed the fortress of Chapultepec (September 13, 1847) and the next day entered Mexico City. Still Mexico refused to negotiate a peace and instead carried on guerilla warfare.

Negotiated peace finally came about when the State Department clerk Nicholas Trist, though his authority had been revoked and he had been ordered back to Washington two

THE MEXICAN WAR

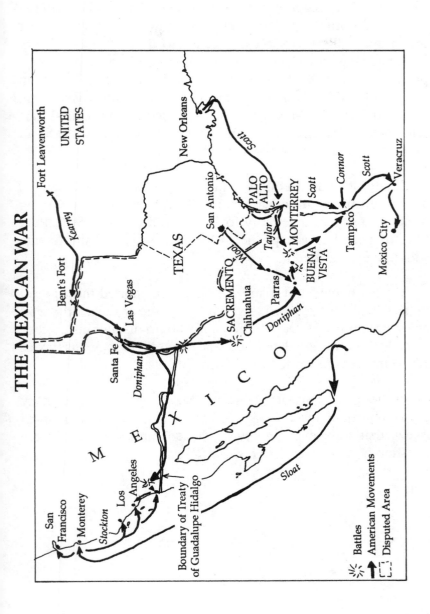

Fort Leavenworth

UNITED STATES

New Orleans

Kearny

Bent's Fort

Las Vegas

Sante Fe

Doniphan

San Antonio

PALO ALTO

Scott

Taylor

Wool

MONTERREY

Connor

Scott

Tampico

Veracruz

BUENA VISTA

Mexico City

TEXAS

SACREMENTO

Chihuahua

Parras

Doniphan

M   E   X   I   C   O

San Francisco

Monterey

Stockton

Los Angeles

Boundary of Treaty of Guadalupe Hidalgo

Sloat

Battles

American Movements

Disputed Area

15

months earlier, negotiated and signed the Treaty of Guadalupe-Hidalgo (February 2, 1848), ending the Mexican War. Under the terms of the treaty Mexico ceded to the U.S. the territory Polk had originally sought to buy, this time in exchange for a payment of $15,000,000 and the assumption of $3,250,000 in American citizens' claims against the Mexican government. This territory, the Mexican Cession, included the natural harbors at San Francisco and San Diego, thus giving the U.S. all three of the major west-coast natural harbors.

Many, including Polk, felt the treaty was far too generous. There had been talk of annexing all of Mexico or of forcing Mexico to pay an indemnity for the cost of the war. Still, Polk felt compelled to accept the treaty as it was, and the Senate subsequently ratified it.

On the home front many Americans supported the war enthusiastically and flocked to volunteer. Some criticized the war, among them Henry David Thoreau, who, to display his protest, went to live at Walden Pond and refused to pay his taxes. Jailed for this, he wrote "Civil Disobedience."

Although the Mexican War increased the nation's territory by one-third, it also brought to the surface serious political issues that threatened to divide the country, particularly the question of slavery in the new territories.

CHAPTER 2

THE CRISIS OF 1850 AND AMERICA AT MID-CENTURY

2.1 THE WILMOT PROVISO

The Mexican War had no more than started when, on August 8, 1846, freshman Democratic Congressman David Wilmot of Pennsylvania introduced his Wilmot Proviso as a proposed amendment to a war appropriations bill. It stipulated that "neither slavery nor involuntary servitude shall ever exist" in any territory to be acquired from Mexico. It was passed by the House, and though rejected by the Senate it was reintroduced again and again amid increasingly acrimonious debate.

The Wilmot Proviso aroused intense sectional feelings. Southerners, who had supported the war enthusiastically, felt they were being treated unfairly. Northerners, some of whom had been inclined to see the war as a slaveholders' plot to extend slavery, felt they saw their worst suspicions confirmed by the southerners' furious opposition to the Wilmot Proviso.

There came to be four views regarding the status of slavery in the newly acquired territories:

1) The southern position was expressed by John C. Calhoun, now serving as senator from South Carolina. He argued that the territories were the property not of the U.S. federal government, but of all the states together, and therefore Congress had no right to prohibit in any territory any type of "property" (by which he meant slaves) that was legal in any of the states.

2) Anti-slavery northerners, pointing to the Northwest Ordinance of 1787 and the Missouri Compromise of 1820 as precedents, argued that Congress had the right to make what laws it saw fit for the territories, including, if it so chose, laws prohibiting slavery.

3) A compromise proposal favored by President Polk and many moderate southerners called for the extension of the 36° 30' line of the Missouri Compromise westward through the Mexican Cession to the Pacific, with territory north of the line to be closed to slavery and territory south of it open to slavery.

4) Another compromise solution, favored by northern Democrats such as Lewis Cass of Michigan and Stephen A. Douglas of Illinois, was known as "squatter sovereignty" and later as "popular sovereignty." It held that the residents of each territory should be permitted to decide for themselves whether or not to allow slavery, but it was vague as to when they might exercise that right.

2.2 THE ELECTION OF 1848

Both parties sought to avoid as much as possible the hot issue of slavery in the territories as they prepared for the 1848 election campaign.

The Democrats nominated Lewis Cass, and their platform endorsed his middle-of-the-road popular sovereignty position with regard to slavery in the territories.

The Whigs dodged the issue even more effectively by nominating General Zachary Taylor, whose fame in the Mexican War made him a strong candidate. Taylor knew nothing of politics, had never voted, and liked to think of himself as above politics. He took no position at all with respect to slavery in the territories.

Some anti-slavery northern Whigs and Democrats, disgusted with their parties' failure to take a clear stand against the spread of slavery, deserted the party ranks to form another anti-slavery third party. They were known as "Conscience" Whigs (because they voted their conscience) and "Barnburner" Democrats (because they were willing to burn down the whole Democratic "barn" to get rid of the pro-slavery "rats"). Their party was called the Free Soil party, since it stood for keeping the soil of new western territories free of slavery. Its candidate was Martin Van Buren.

The election excited relatively little public interest. Taylor won a narrow victory, apparently because Van Buren took enough votes from Cass in New York and Pennsylvania to throw those states into Taylor's column.

2.3 GOLD IN CALIFORNIA

The question of slavery's status in the western territories was made more immediate when, on January 24, 1848, gold was discovered at Sutter's Mill, not far from Sacramento, California. The next year gold-seekers from the eastern U.S. and from many foreign countries swelled California's population from 14,000 to 100,000.

Once in the gold fields these "forty-niners" proved to contain some rough characters, and that fact, along with the presence, or at least the expectation, of quick and easy riches, made California a wild and lawless place. No territorial government had been organized since the U.S. had received the land as part of the Mexican Cession, and all that existed was an inadequate military government. In September 1849, having more than the requisite population and being much in need of better government, California petitioned for admission to the Union as a state.

Since few slaveholders had chosen to risk their valuable investments in human property in the turbulent atmosphere of California, the people of the area not surprisingly sought admission as a free state, touching off a serious sectional crisis back east.

2.4   THE COMPROMISE OF 1850

President Zachary Taylor, though himself a Louisiana slaveholder, opposed the further spread of slavery. Hoping to sidestep the dangerously devisive issue of slavery in the territories, he encouraged California as well as the rest of the Mexican Cession to organize and seek admission directly as states, thus completely bypassing the territorial stage.

Southerners were furious. They saw admission of a free-state California as a back-door implementation of the hated Wilmot Proviso they had fought so hard to turn back in Congress. They were also growing increasingly alarmed at what was becoming the minority status of their section within the country. Long outnumbered in the House of Representatives, the South would now find itself, should California be admitted as a free state, also outvoted in the Senate.

Other matters created friction between North and South. A large tract of land was disputed between Texas, a slave state, and the as yet unorganized New Mexico Territory, where slavery's future was at best uncertain. Southerners were angered by the small-scale but much talked of efforts of northern abolitionists' "underground railroad" to aid escaped slaves in reaching permanent freedom in Canada. Northerners were disgusted by the presence of slave pens and slave markets in the nation's capital. Radical southerners talked of secession and scheduled an all-southern convention to meet in Nashville in June 1850 to propose ways of protecting southern interests, inside or outside the Union.

At this point the aged Henry Clay attempted to compromise the various matters of contention between North and South. He proposed an eight-part package deal that he hoped would appeal to both sides:

For the North, the package contained these aspects:

1) California would be admitted as a free state.

2) The land in dispute between Texas and New Mexico would go to New Mexico.

3) New Mexico and Utah Territories (all of the Mexican Cession outside of California) would not be specifically reserved for slavery, but its status there would be decided by popular sovereignty.

4) The slave trade would be abolished in the District of Columbia.

For the South, the package offered the following:

1) A tougher Fugitive Slave Law would be enacted.

2) The federal government would pay Texas' $10,000,000 pre-annexation debt.

3) Congress would declare that it did not have jurisdiction over the interstate slave trade.

4) Congress would promise not to abolish slavery itself in the District of Columbia.

What followed the introduction of Clay's compromise proposal was eight months of heated debate, during which Clay, Calhoun, and Daniel Webster, the three great figures of Congress during the first half of the nineteenth century — all three aged and none of them with more than two years to live — made some of their greatest speeches. Clay called for compromise and "mutual forbearance." Calhoun gravely warned that the only way to save the Union was for the North to grant all the South's demands and keep quiet on the issue of slavery. Webster abandoned his previous opposition to the spread of slavery (as well as most of his popularity back in his home state of Massachusetts) to support the Compromise in an eloquent speech.

The opponents of the Compromise were many and powerful and ranged from President Taylor, who demanded admission of California without reference to slavery, to northern extremists such as Senator William Seward of New York, who spoke of a "higher law" than the Constitution, forbidding the spread of slavery, to southern extremists such as Calhoun or Senator Jefferson Davis of Mississippi. By mid-summer all seemed lost for the Compromise, and Clay left Washington exhausted and discouraged.

Then the situation changed dramatically. President Taylor died (apparently of gastroenteritis) July 9, 1850, and was succeeded by Vice President Millard Fillmore, a quiet but efficient politician and a strong supporter of compromise. In Congress the fight for the Compromise was taken up by Senator Stephen A. Douglas of Illinois. Called the "Little Giant" for his small stature but large political skills, Douglas broke Clay's proposal into its component parts so that he could use varying coalitions to push each part through Congress. This method proved successful, and the Compromise was adopted.

The Compromise of 1850 was received with joy by most of the nation. Sectional harmony returned, for the most part, and the issue of slavery in the territories seemed to have been permanently settled. That this was an illusion became apparent within a few years.

2.5   THE ELECTION OF 1852

The 1852 Democratic convention deadlocked between Cass and Douglas and so instead settled on dark horse Franklin Pierce of New Hampshire.

The Whigs, true to form, chose General Winfield Scott, a war hero of no political background.

The result was an easy victory for Pierce, largely because the Whig party, badly divided along North-South lines as a result of the battle over the Compromise of 1850, was beginning to come apart.

The Free Soil party's candidate, John P. Hale of New Hampshire, fared poorly, demonstrating the electorate's weariness with the slavery issue.

2.6   PIERCE AND "YOUNG AMERICA"

Americans eagerly turned their attention to railroads, cotton, clipper ships, and commerce. The world seemed to be opening up to American trade and influence.

President Pierce expressed the nation's hope that a new era of sectional peace was beginning. To assure this he sought to distract the nation's attention from the slavery issue to an aggressive program of foreign economic and territorial expansion known as "Young America."

In 1853 Commodore Matthew Perry led a U.S. naval force into Tokyo Bay on a peaceful mission to open Japan — previously closed to the outside world — to American diplomacy and commerce.

By means of the Reciprocity Treaty (1854) Pierce succeeded in opening Canada to greater U.S. trade. He also sought to annex Hawaii, increase U.S. interest in Central America, and acquire territories from Mexico and Spain.

From Mexico he acquired in 1853 the Gadsden Purchase, a strip of land in what is now southern New Mexico and Arizona along the Gila River. The purpose of this purchase was to provide a good route for a trans-continental railroad across the southern part of the country.

Pierce sought to buy Cuba from Spain. When Spain declined, three of Pierce's diplomats, meeting in Ostend, Belgium, sent him the Ostend Manifesto urging military seizure of Cuba should Spain remain intransigent.

Pierce was the first "doughface" president — "a northern

EXPANSION OF THE UNITED STATES

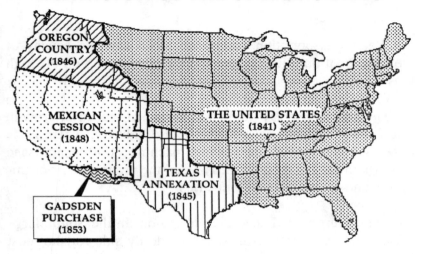

man with southern principles" — and his expansionist goals, situated as they were in the South, aroused suspicion and hostility in anti-slavery northerners. Pierce's administration appeared to be dominated by southerners, such as Secretary of War Jefferson Davis, and whether in seeking a southern route for a trans-continental railroad or seeking to annex potential slave territory such as Cuba, it seemed to be working for the good of the South.

2.7   ECONOMIC GROWTH

The chief factor in the economic transformation of America during the 1840s and 1850s was the dynamic rise of the railroads. In 1840 America had less than 3000 miles of railroad track. By 1860 that number had risen to over 30,000 miles. Railroads pioneered big-business techniques, and by improving transportation helped create a nationwide market. They also helped link the Midwest to the Northeast rather than the South, as would have been the case had only water transportation been available.

Water transportation during the 1850s saw the heyday of the steamboat on inland rivers and the clipper ship on the high seas.

The period also saw rapid and sustained industrial growth. The factory system began in the textile industry, where Elias Howe's invention of the sewing machine (1846) and Isaac Singer's improved model (1851) aided the process of mechanization, and spread to other industries.

Agriculture varied according to region. In the South, large plantations and small farms existed side by side for the most part, and both prospered enormously during the 1850s from the production of cotton. Southern leaders referred to the fiber as "King Cotton," an economic power that no one would dare fight against.

In the North the main centers of agricultural production shifted from the Middle Atlantic states to the more fertile lands of the Midwest. The main unit of agriculture was the family farm, and the main products were grain and livestock. Unlike the South where 3,500,000 slaves provided abundant labor, the North faced incentives to introduce labor-saving machines. Cyrus McCormick's mechanical reaper came into wide use, and by 1860 over 100,000 were in operation on Midwestern farms. Mechanical threshers also came into increasing use.

2.8 DECLINE OF THE TWO PARTY SYSTEM

Meanwhile, ominous developments were taking place in politics. America's second two-party system, which had developed during the 1830s, was in the process of breaking down. The Whig party, whose dismal performance in the election of 1852 had signaled its weakness, was now in the process of complete disintegration. Partially this was the result of the issue of slavery, which tended to divide the party along North-South lines. Partially, though, it may have been the result of the nativist movement.

The nativist movement and its political party, the American, or, as it was called, the Know-Nothing party, grew out of alarm on the part of native-born Americans at the rising tide of German and Irish immigration during the late 1840s and early 1850s. The Know-Nothing party, so called because its members were told to answer "I know nothing" when asked about its secret proceedings, was anti-foreign and, since many of the foreigners were Catholic, also anti-Catholic. It surged briefly to become the country's second largest party by 1855 but faded even more quickly due to the ineptness of its leaders and the growing urgency of the slavery question, which, though ignored by the Know-Nothing party, was rapidly coming to overshadow all other issues. To some extent the Know-Nothing movement may simply have benefitted from the already progressing disintegration of the Whig party, but it may also have helped to complete that disintegration.

All of this was ominous because the collapse of a viable nationwide two-party system made it much more difficult for the nation's political process to contain the explosive issue of slavery.

CHAPTER 3

THE RETURN OF SECTIONAL CONFLICT

3.1 CONTINUING SOURCES OF TENSION

While Americans hailed the apparent sectional harmony created by the Compromise of 1850 and enjoyed the rapid economic growth of the decade that followed, two items which continued to create tension centered on the issue of slavery.

3.1.1 *The Strengthened Fugitive Slave Law*

The more important of these was a part of the Compromise itself, the strengthened federal Fugitive Slave Law. The law enraged northerners, many of whom believed it little better than a legalization of kidnapping. Under its provisions blacks living in the North and claimed by slave catchers were denied trial by jury and many of the other protections of due process. Even more distasteful to anti-slavery northerners was the provision that required all U.S. citizens to aid, when called upon, in the capture and return of alleged fugitives. So violent was northern feeling against the law that several riots erupted as a result of attempts to enforce it. Some northern states passed personal liberty laws in an attempt to prevent the working of the Fugitive Slave Law.

The effect of all this was to polarize the country even further. Many northerners who had not previously taken an interest in the slavery issue now became opponents of slavery as a result of having its injustices forcibly brought home to them by the Fugitive Slave Law. Southerners saw in northern resistance to the law further proof that the North was determined to tamper with the institution of slavery.

3.1.2 *Publishing of* Uncle Tom's Cabin

One northerner who was outraged by the Fugitive Slave Act was Harriet Beecher Stowe. In response, she wrote *Uncle Tom's Cabin*, a fictional book depicting what she perceived as the evils of slavery. Furiously denounced in the South, the book became an overnight bestseller in the North, where it turned many toward active opposition to slavery. This, too, was a note of harsh discord among the seemingly harmonious sectional relations of the early 1850s.

3.2   THE KANSAS-NEBRASKA ACT

All illusion of sectional peace ended abruptly when in 1854 Senator Stephen A. Douglas of Illinois introduced a bill in Congress to organize the area west of Missouri and Iowa as the territories of Kansas and Nebraska. Douglas, who apparently had no moral convictions on slavery one way or the other, hoped organizing the territories would facilitate the building of a trans-continental railroad on a central route, something that would benefit him and his Illinois constituents.

Though he sought to avoid directly addressing the touchy issue of slavery, Douglas was compelled by pressure from south-

FREE AND SLAVE AREAS, 1854

ern senators such as David Atchison of Missouri to include in the bill an explicit repeal of the Missouri Compromise (which banned slavery in the areas in question) and a provision that the status of slavery in the newly organized territories be decided by popular sovereignty.

The bill was opposed by most northern Democrats and a majority of the remaining Whigs, but with the support of the southern-dominated Pierce administration it was passed and signed into law.

3.3   THE REPUBLICAN PARTY

The Kansas-Nebraska Act aroused a storm of outrage in the North, where the repeal of the Missouri Compromise was seen as the breaking of a solemn agreement. It hastened the disintegration of the Whig party and divided the Democratic party along North-South lines.

In the North, many Democrats left the party and were joined by former Whigs and Know-Nothings in the newly created Republican party. Springing to life almost overnight as a result of northern fury at the Kansas-Nebraska Act, the Republican party included diverse elements whose sole unifying principle was the firm belief that slavery should be banned from all the nation's territories, confined to the states where it already existed, and allowed to spread no further.

Though its popularity was confined almost entirely to the North, the Republican Party quickly became a major power in national politics.

3.4   BLEEDING KANSAS

With the status of Kansas (Nebraska was never in much doubt) to be decided by the voters there, North and South began competing to see which could send the greatest number. Northerners formed the New England Emigrant Aid Company to promote the settling of anti-slavery men in Kansas, and southerners responded in kind. Despite these efforts the majority of Kansas settlers were midwesterners who were generally opposed to the spread of slavery but were more concerned with finding good farm land than deciding the national debate over slavery in the territories.

Despite this large anti-slavery majority, large-scale election fraud, especially on the part of heavily armed Missouri "border ruffians" who crossed into Kansas on election day to vote their pro-slavery principles early and often, led to the creation of a virulently pro-slavery territorial government. When the Presidentially appointed territorial governor protested this gross fraud, Pierce removed him from office.

Free-soil Kansans responded by denouncing the pro-slavery government as illegitimate and forming their own free-soil government in an election which the pro-slavery faction boycotted. Kansas now had two rival governments, each claiming to be the only lawful one.

Both sides began arming themselves and soon the territory was being referred to in the northern press as "Bleeding Kansas" as full-scale guerilla war erupted. In May 1856, Missouri border ruffians sacked the free-soil town of Lawrence, killing two, and destroying homes, businesses, and printing presses. Two days later a small band of anti-slavery zealots under the leadership of fanatical abolitionist John Brown retaliated by killing and mutilating five unarmed men and boys at a pro-slavery settlement on Pottawatomie Creek. In all, some 200 died in the months of guerilla fighting that followed.

Meanwhile, violence had spread even to Congress itself. In the same month as the Sack of Lawrence and the Pottawatomie Massacre, Senator Charles Sumner of Massachusetts made a two-day speech entitled "The Crime Against Kansas," in which he not only denounced slavery but also made degrading personal references to aged South Carolina Senator Andrew Butler. Two days later Butler's nephew, Congressman Preston Brooks, also of South Carolina, entered the Senate chamber and, coming on Sumner from behind, beat him about the head and shoulders with a cane, leaving him bloody and unconscious.

Once again the North was outraged, while in the South, Brooks was hailed as a hero. New canes were sent to him to replace the one he had broken over Sumner's head. Denounced by northerners, he resigned his seat and was overwhelmingly re-elected. Northerners were further incensed and bought thousands of copies of Sumner's inflammatory speech.

3.5   THE ELECTION OF 1856

The election of 1856 was a three-way contest that pitted Democrats, Know-Nothings, and Republicans against each other.

The Democrats dropped Pierce and passed over Douglas to nominate James Buchanan of Pennsylvania. Though a veteran of forty years of politics, Buchanan was a weak and vacillating man whose chief qualification for the nomination was that during the slavery squabbles of the past few years he had been out of the country as American minister to Great Britain and therefore had not been forced to take public positions on the controversial issues.

The Know-Nothings, including the remnant of the Whigs, nominated Millard Fillmore. However, choice of a southerner for the nomination of Vice-President so alienated northern Know-Nothings that many shifted their support to the Republican candidate.

The Republicans nominated John C. Frémont of California. A former officer in the army's Corps of Topographical Engineers, Frémont was known as "the Pathfinder" for his explorations in the Rockies and the Far West. The Republican platform called for high tariffs, free western homesteads (160 acres) for settlers, and, most important, no further spread of slavery. Their slogan was "Free Soil, Free Men, and Frémont." Southerners denounced the Republican party as an abolitionist organization and threatened secession should it win the election.

Against divided opposition Buchanan won with apparent ease. However, his victory was largely based on the support of the South, since Frémont carried most of the northern states. Had the Republicans won Pennsylvania and either Illinois or Indiana, Frémont would have been elected. In the election the

Republicans demonstrated surprising strength for a political party only two years old and made clear that they, and not the Know-Nothings, would replace the moribund Whigs as the other major party along with the Democrats.

3.6   THE DRED SCOTT CASE

Meanwhile, there had been rising through the court system a case that would give the Supreme Court a chance to state its opinion on the question of slavery in the territories. The case was *Dred Scott v. Sanford* and involved a Missouri slave, Dred Scott, who had been encouraged by abolitionists to sue for his freedom on the basis that his owner, an army doctor, had taken him for a stay of several years in a free state, Illinois, and then in a free territory, Wisconsin. By 1856 the case had made its way to the Supreme Court, and by March of the following year the Court was ready to render its decision.

The justices were at first inclined to rule simply that Scott, as a slave, was not a citizen and could not sue in court. Buchanan, however, shortly before his inauguration urged the justices to go farther and attempt to settle the whole slavery issue once and for all, thus removing it from the realm of politics where it might prove embarrassing to the President.

The Court obliged. Under the domination of aging prosouthern Chief Justice Roger B. Taney of Maryland, it attempted to read the extreme southern position on slavery into the Constitution, ruling not only that Scott had no standing to sue in federal court, but also that temporary residence in a free state, even for several years, did not make a slave free, and that the Missouri Compromise (already a dead letter by that time) had been unconstitutional all along because Congress did not have the authority to exclude slavery from any territory whatsoever. Nor did territorial governments, which were considered to receive their power from Congress, have the right to prohibit slavery.

Far from settling the sectional controversy, the Dred Scott case only made it worse. Southerners were encouraged to take an extreme position and refuse compromise, while anti-slavery northerners became more convinced than ever that there was a pro-slavery conspiracy controlling all branches of government, and expressed an unwillingness to accept the Court's dictate as final.

3.7 BUCHANAN AND KANSAS

Later in 1857 the proslavery government in Kansas, through largely fraudulent means, arranged for a heavily pro-slavery constitutional convention to meet at the town of Lecompton. The result was a state constitution that allowed slavery. To obtain a pretense of popular approval for this constitution the convention provided for a referendum in which the voters were to be given a choice only to prohibit the entry of additional slaves into the state.

Disgusted free-soilers boycotted the referendum, and the result was a constitution that put no restrictions at all on slavery. Touting this Lecompton constitution, the pro-slavery territorial government petitioned Congress for admission to the Union as a slave state. Meanwhile the free-soilers drafted a constitution of their own and submitted it to Congress as the legitimate one for the prospective state of Kansas.

Eager to appease the South, which had started talking of secession again, and equally eager to suppress anti-slavery agitation in the North, Buchanan vigorously backed the Lecompton constitution. Douglas, appalled at this travesty of popular sovereignty, broke with the administration to oppose it. He and

Buchanan became bitter political enemies, with the President determined to use all the power of the Democratic organization to crush Douglas politically.

After extremely bitter and acrimonious debate the Senate approved the Lecompton constitution, but the House insisted that Kansans be given a chance to vote on the entire document. Southern Congressmen did succeed in managing to apply pressure to the Kansas voters by adding the stipulation that should the Lecompton constitution be approved, Kansas would receive a generous grant of federal land, but should it be voted down, Kansas would remain a territory.

Nevertheless, Kansas voters, when given a chance to express themselves in a fair election, turned down the Lecompton constitution by an overwhelming margin, choosing to remain a territory rather than become a slave state. Kansas was finally admitted as a free state in 1861.

3.8   THE PANIC OF 1857

In 1857 the country was struck by a short but severe depression. There were three basic causes for this "Panic of 1857":

1) several years of overspeculation in railroads and lands,

2) faulty banking practices, and

3) an interruption in the flow of European capital into American investments as a result of the Crimean War.

The North blamed the Panic on low tariffs, while the South, which had suffered much less than the industrial North, saw the Panic as proof of the superiority of the southern economy in general and slavery in particular.

3.9   THE LINCOLN-DOUGLAS DEBATES

The 1858 Illinois senatorial campaign produced a series of debates that got to the heart of the issues that were threatening to divide the nation. In that race incumbent Democratic Senator and front-runner for the 1860 presidential nomination Stephen A. Douglas was opposed by a Springfield lawyer, little known outside the state, by the name of Abraham Lincoln.

Though Douglas had been hailed in some free-soil circles for his opposition to the Lecompton constitution, Lincoln, in a series of seven debates that the candidates agreed to hold during the course of the campaign, stressed that Douglas's doctrine of popular sovereignty failed to recognize slavery for the moral wrong it was. Again and again Lincoln hammered home the theme that Douglas was a secret defender of slavery because he did not take a moral stand against it.

Douglas, for his part, maintained that his guiding principle was democracy, not any moral standard of right or wrong with respect to slavery. The people could, as far as he was concerned, "vote it up or vote it down." At the same time he strove to depict Lincoln as a radical and an abolitionist who believed in racial equality and race mixing.

At the debate held in Freeport, Illinois, Lincoln pressed Douglas to reconcile the principle of popular sovereignty to the Supreme Court's decision in the Dred Scott Case. How could the people "vote it up or vote it down," if, as the Supreme Court alleged, no territorial government could prohibit slavery? Douglas, in what came to be called his "Freeport Doctrine," replied that the people of any territory could exclude slavery simply by declining to pass any of the special laws that slave jurisdictions usually passed for their protection.

Douglas's answer was good enough to win him re-election to the Senate, although by the narrowest of margins, but hurt him in the coming presidential campaign. The Lecompton fight had already destroyed Douglas's hopes of uniting the Democratic party and defusing the slave issue. It had also damaged his 1860 presidential hopes by alienating the South. Now his Freeport Doctrine hardened the opposition of southerners already angered by his anti-Lecompton stand.

For Lincoln, despite the failure to win the Senate seat, the debates were a major success, propelling him into the national spotlight and strengthening the backbone of the Republican party to resist compromise on the free-soil issue.

CHAPTER 4

THE COMING OF
THE CIVIL WAR

4.1   JOHN BROWN'S RAID

On the night of October 16, 1859, John Brown, the Potta-watomie Creek murderer, led eighteen followers in seizing the federal arsenal at Harpers Ferry, Virginia (now West Virginia), taking hostages, and endeavoring to incite a slave uprising.

Brown, supported and bankrolled by several prominent northern abolitionists (later referred to as "the Secret Six"), planned to arm local slaves and then spread his uprising across the South. His scheme was ill-conceived and had little chance of success. Quickly cornered by Virginia militia, he was eventually captured by a force of U.S. Marines under the command of Army Colonel Robert E. Lee. Ten of Brown's eighteen men were killed in the fight, and Brown himself was wounded.

Charged under Virginia law with treason and various other crimes, Brown was quickly tried, convicted, sentenced, and, on December 2, 1859, hanged. Throughout his trial and at his execution he conducted himself with fanatical resolution, making eloquent and grandiose statements that convinced many northerners that he was a martyr rather than a criminal. His death was marked in the North by signs of public mourning.

Though responsible northerners such as Lincoln denounced Brown's raid as a criminal act that deserved to be punished by death, many southerners became convinced that the entire northern public approved of Brown's action and that the only safety for the South lay in a separate southern confederacy. This was all the more so because Brown, in threatening to create a slave revolt, had touched on the foremost fear of white southerners.

4.2   HINTON ROWAN HELPER'S BOOK

The second greatest fear of southern slaveholders was that southern whites who did not own slaves, by far the majority of the southern population, would come to see the continuation of slavery as not being in their best interest. This fear was touched on by a book, *The Impending Crisis in the South*, by a North Carolinian named Hinton Rowan Helper. In it Helper argued that slavery was economically harmful to the South and that it enriched the large planter at the expense of the yeoman farmer.

Southerners were enraged, and more so when the Republicans reissued a condensed version of the book as campaign literature. When the new House of Representatives met in December 1859 for the first time since the 1858 elections, angry southerners determined that no Republican who had endorsed the book should be elected speaker.

The Republicans were the most numerous party in the House although they did not hold a majority. Their candidate for speaker, John Sherman of Ohio, had endorsed Helper's book. A rancorous two-month battle ensued in which the House was unable even to organize itself, let alone transact any business.

Secession was talked of openly by southerners, and as tensions rose Congressmen came to the sessions carrying revolvers and Bowie knives. The matter was finally resolved by the withdrawal of Sherman and the election of a moderate Republican as speaker. Tensions remained fairly high.

4.3   THE ELECTION OF 1860

In this mood the country approached the election of 1860, a campaign that eventually became a four-man contest.

The Democrats met in Charleston, South Carolina. Douglas had a majority of the delegates, but at that time a party rule required a two-thirds vote for the nomination. Douglas, faced with the bitter opposition of the southerners and the Buchanan faction, could not gain this majority. Finally, the convention split up when southern "fire-eaters" led by William L. Yancey walked out in protest of the convention's refusal to include in the platform a plank demanding federal protection of slavery in all the territories.

A second Democratic convention several weeks later in Baltimore also failed to reach a consensus, and the sundered halves of the party nominated separate candidates.

The southern wing of the party nominated Buchanan's vice president, John C. Breckinridge of Kentucky, on a platform calling for a federal slave code in all the territories.

What was left of the national Democratic party nominated Douglas on a platform of popular sovereignty.

A third presidential candidate was added by the Constitutional Union party, a collection of aging former Whigs and Know Nothings from the southern and border states as well as a handful of moderate southern Democrats. It nominated John Bell of Tennessee on a platform that sidestepped the issues and called simply for the Constitution, the Union, and the enforcement of the laws.

The Republicans met in Chicago, confident of victory and determined to do nothing to jeopardize their favorable position. Accordingly they rejected as too radical front-running New York Senator William H. Seward in favor of Illinois favorite son Abraham Lincoln. The platform was designed to have something for all northerners, including the provisions of the 1856 Republican platform as well as a call for federal support of a trans-continental railroad. Once again its centerpiece was a call for the containment of slavery.

Douglas, believing only his victory could reconcile North and South, became the first U.S. Presidential candidate to make a vigorous nationwide speaking tour. In his speeches he urged support for the Union and opposition to any extremist candidates that might endanger its survival, by which he meant Lincoln and Breckinridge.

On election day the voting went along strictly sectional lines. Breckinridge carried the Deep South; Bell, the border states; and Lincoln, the North. Douglas, although second in popular votes, carried only a single state and part of another. Lincoln led in popular votes, and though he was short of a majority in that category, he did have the needed majority in electoral votes and was elected.

4.4   THE SECESSION CRISIS

Lincoln had declared he had no intention of disturbing slavery where it already existed, but many southerners thought otherwise. They also feared further raids of the sort John Brown had attempted and felt their pride injured by the election of a President for whom no southerner had voted.

On December 20, 1860, South Carolina, by vote of a special convention made up of delegates elected by the people of the state, declared itself out of the Union. By February 1, 1861, six more states (Alabama, Georgia, Florida, Mississippi, Louisiana, and Texas) had followed suit.

Representatives of the seven seceded states met in Montgomery, Alabama, in February 1861 and declared themselves to be the Confederate States of America. They elected former Secretary of War and U.S. Senator Jefferson Davis of Mississippi as president, and Alexander Stephens of Georgia as vice president. They also adopted a constitution for the Confederate States which, while similar to the U.S. Constitution in many ways, contained several important differences:

1) Slavery was specifically recognized, and the right to move slaves from one state to another was guaranteed.

2) Protective tariffs were prohibited.

3) The president was to serve for a single non-renewable six-year term.

4) The president was given the right to veto individual items within an appropriations bill.

5) State sovereignty was specifically recognized.

In the North reaction was mixed. Some, such as prominent Republican Horace Greeley of the New York *Tribune*, counseled, "Let erring sisters go in peace." President Buchanan, now a lame duck, seemed to be of this mind, since he declared

FREE AND SLAVE AREAS, 1861

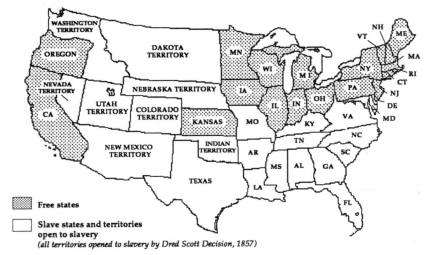

Free states

Slave states and territories
open to slavery
(all territories opened to slavery by Dred Scott Decision, 1857)

secession to be unconstitutional but at the same time stated his belief that it was unconstitutional for the federal government to do anything to stop states from seceding. Taking his own advice, he did nothing.

Others, led by Senator John J. Crittenden of Kentucky, strove for a compromise that would preserve the Union. Throughout the period of several weeks as the southern states one by one declared their secession, Crittenden worked desperately with a Congressional compromise committee in hopes of working out some form of agreement.

The compromise proposals centered on the passage of a constitutional amendment forever prohibiting federal meddling with slavery in the states where it existed as well as the extension of the Missouri Compromise line (36° 30') to the Pacific, with slavery specifically protected in all the territories south of it.

Some Congressional Republicans were inclined to accept this compromise, but President-elect Lincoln urged them to stand firm for no further spread of slavery. Southerners would consider no compromise that did not provide for the spread of slavery, and talks broke down.

4.5   FORT SUMTER

Lincoln did his best to avoid angering the slave states that had not yet seceded. In his inaugural address he urged southerners to reconsider their actions but warned that the Union was perpetual, that states could not secede, and that he would therefore hold the federal forts and installations in the South.

Of these only two remained in Federal hands: Fort Pickens, off Pensacola, Florida; and Fort Sumter, in the harbor of Charleston, South Carolina. Lincoln soon received word from Major Robert Anderson, commanding the small garrison at Sumter, that supplies were running low. Desiring to send in the needed supplies, Lincoln informed the governor of South Carolina of his intention but promised that no attempt would be made to send arms, ammunition, or reinforcements unless southerners initiated hostilities.

Not satisfied, southerners determined to take the fort. Confederate General P. G. T. Beauregard, acting on orders from President Davis, demanded Anderson's surrender. Anderson said he would if not resupplied. Knowing supplies were on the way, the Confederates opened fire at 4:30 a.m. on April 12, 1861. The next day the fort surrendered.

The day following Sumter's surrender Lincoln declared the existence of an insurrection and called for the states to provide 75,000 volunteers to put it down. In response to this, Virginia,

Tennessee, North Carolina, and Arkansas declared their secession.

The remaining slave states, Delaware, Kentucky, Maryland, and Missouri, wavered to varying degrees but stayed with the Union:

1) Delaware, which had few slaves, gave little serious consideration to the idea of secession.

2) Kentucky declared itself neutral and then sided with the North when the South failed to respect this neutrality.

3) Maryland's incipient secession movement was crushed by Lincoln's timely imposition of martial law.

4) Missouri was saved for the Union by the quick and decisive use of Federal troops as well as the sizeable population of pro-Union, anti-slavery German immigrants living in St. Louis.

4.6   RELATIVE STRENGTHS AT THE OUTSET

An assessment of available assets at the beginning of the war would not have looked favorable for the South.

The North enjoyed at least five major advantages over the South:

1) The North had overwhelming preponderance in wealth and thus was better able to finance the enormous expense of the war.

2) The North was also vastly superior in industry and thus

capable of producing the needed war materials; while the South, as a primarily agricultural society, often had to improvise or do without.

3) The North had an advantage of almost three to one in manpower; and over one-third of the South's population was composed of slaves, whom southerners would not use as soldiers. Unlike the South, the North received large numbers of immigrants during the war.

4) The North retained control of the U.S. Navy, and thus would command the sea and be able, by blockading, to cut the South off from outside sources of supply.

5) Finally, the North enjoyed a much superior system of railroads, while the South's relatively sparse railroad net was composed of a number of smaller railroads, often not interconnected and with varying gauges of track, more useful for carrying cotton from the interior to port cities than for moving large amounts of war supplies or troops around the country.

The South did, however, have several advantages of its own:

1) It was vast in size, and this would make it difficult to conquer.

2) It did not need to conquer the North, but only resist being conquered itself.

3) Its troops would be fighting on their own ground, a fact that would give them the advantage of familiarity with the terrain as well as the added motivation of defending their homes and families.

4) Its armies would often have the opportunity of fighting on the defensive, a major advantage in the warfare of that day.

5) At the outset of the war the South drew a number of highly qualified senior officers, such as Robert E. Lee, Joseph E. Johnston, and Albert Sidney Johnston, from the U.S. Army. By contrast, the Union command structure was already set when the war began, with the aged Winfield Scott, of Mexican War fame, at the top. It took young and talented officers, such as Ulysses S. Grant and William T. Sherman, time to work up to high rank. Meanwhile Union armies were often led by inferior commanders as Lincoln experimented in search of good generals.

At first glance, the South might also have seemed to have an advantage in its president. Jefferson Davis had extensive military and political experience and was acquainted with the nation's top military men and, presumably, with their relative abilities. On the other hand, Lincoln had been, up until his election to the presidency, less successfully politically and had virtually no military experience. In fact, Lincoln was much superior to Davis as a war leader, showing firmness, flexibility, mental toughness, great political skill, and, eventually, an excellent grasp of strategy.

4.7 OPPOSING STRATEGIES

Both sides were full of enthusiasm for the war. In the North the battle cry was "On to Richmond," the new Confederate capital established after the secession of Virginia. In the South it was "On to Washington." Yielding to popular demand, Lincoln ordered General Irvin McDowell to advance on Richmond with his army. At a creek called Bull Run near the town of

Manassas Junction, Virginia, just southwest of Washington, D.C., they met a Confederate force under generals P.G.T. Beauregard and Joseph E. Johnston, July 21, 1861. In the First Battle of Bull Run (called First Manassas in the South) the Union army was forced to retreat in confusion back to Washington.

Bull Run demonstrated the unpreparedness and inexperience of both sides. It also demonstrated that the war would be long and hard, and, particularly in the North, that greater efforts would be required. Lincoln would need an overall strategy. To supply this, Winfield Scott suggested his Anaconda Plan to squeeze the life out of the Confederacy:

1) A naval blockade to shut out supplies from Europe,

2) A campaign to take the Mississippi River, splitting the South in two, and

3) Taking a few strategic points and waiting for pro-Union sentiment in the South to overthrow the secessionists.

Lincoln liked the first two points of Scott's strategy but considered the third point unrealistic.

He ordered a naval blockade, an overwhelming task considering the South's long coastline. Yet under Secretary of the Navy Gideon Welles the Navy was expanded enormously and the blockade, derided in the early days as a "paper blockade," became increasingly effective.

Lincoln also ordered a campaign to take the Mississippi River. A major step in this direction was taken when naval forces under Captain David G. Farragut took New Orleans in April 1862.

Rather than waiting for pro-Unionists in the South to gain control, Lincoln hoped to raise huge armies and apply overwhelming pressure from all sides at once until the Confederacy collapsed. The strategy was good; the problem was finding good generals to carry it out.

CHAPTER 5

THE UNION PRESERVED

5.1 LINCOLN TRIES McCLELLAN

To replace the discredited McDowell, Lincoln chose General George B. McClellan. McClellan was a good trainer and organizer and was loved by the troops, but was unable to use effectively the powerful army (now called the Army of the Potomac) he had built up. Despite much prodding from Lincoln, McClellan hesitated to advance, badly overestimating his enemy's numbers.

Finally, in the spring of 1862, he took the Army of the Potomac by water down Chesapeake Bay to land between the York and James Rivers in Virginia. His plan was to advance up the peninsula formed by these rivers directly to Richmond.

The operations that followed were known as the Peninsula Campaign. McClellan advanced slowly and cautiously toward Richmond, while his equally cautious Confederate opponent, General Joseph E. Johnston, drew back to the outskirts of the city before turning to fight at the Battle of Seven Pines. In this inconclusive battle Johnston was wounded. To replace him Jefferson Davis appointed his military advisor, General Robert E. Lee.

Lee summoned General Thomas J. "Stonewall" Jackson and his army from the Shenandoah Valley (where Jackson had just finished defeating several superior Federal forces, causing consternation in Washington) and with the combined forces attacked McClellan.

After two days of bloody but inconclusive fighting, McClellan lost his nerve and began to retreat. In the remainder of what came to be called the Battle of the Seven Days, Lee continued to attack McClellan, forcing him back to his base, though at great cost in lives. McClellan's army was loaded back onto its ships and taken back to Washington.

Before McClellan's army could reach Washington and be completely deployed in northern Virginia, Lee saw and took an opportunity to thrash Union General John Pope, who was operating in northern Virginia with another northern army, at the Second Battle of Bull Run.

5.2 UNION VICTORIES IN THE WEST

In the western area of the war's operations, essentially everything west of the Appalachian Mountains, matters were proceeding in a much different fashion. The northern commanders there, Henry W. Halleck and Don Carlos Buell, were no more enterprising than McClellan, but Halleck's subordinate, Ulysses S. Grant, definitely was.

Seeking and obtaining permission from Halleck, Grant mounted a combined operation — army troops and navy gun-

MAJOR MILITARY OPERATIONS, 1862

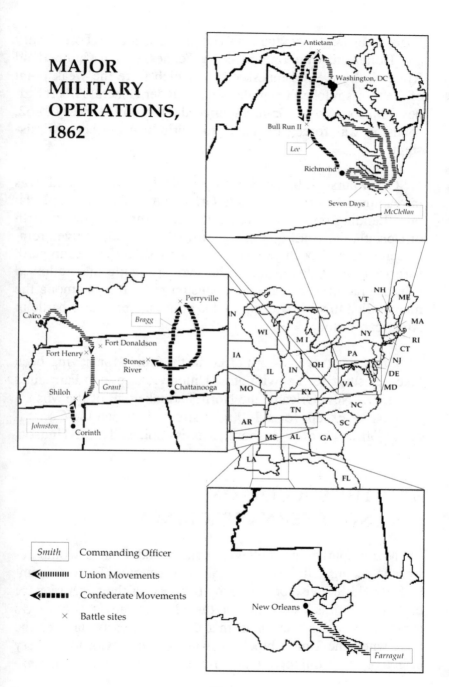

Antietam

Washington, DC

Bull Run II ×

Lee

Richmond●

Seven Days

McClellan

Perryville ×

Cairo

Bragg

× Fort Donaldson

Fort Henry ×

Stones × River

Grant

Chattanooga ●

Shiloh ×

Johnston

● Corinth

NH

VT

ME

MA

NY

RI

CT

PA

NJ

DE

MD

VA

N

WI

M I

IA

IL

IN

OH

MO

KY

NC

TN

AR

SC

MS

AL

GA

LA

FL

New Orleans ●

Farragut

Smith   Commanding Officer

◀▥▥▥▥▥   Union Movements

◀■■■■■   Confederate Movements

×   Battle sites

boats — against two vital Confederate strongholds, Forts Henry and Donelson, which guarded the Tennessee and Cumberland Rivers in northern Tennessee, and which were the weak point of the thin-stretched Confederate line under General Albert Sidney Johnson. When Grant captured the forts in February 1862, Johnston was forced to retreat to Corinth in northern Mississippi.

Grant pursued but, ordered by Halleck to wait until all was in readiness before proceeding, Grant halted his troops at Pittsburg Landing on the Tennessee River, twenty-five miles north of Corinth. On April 6, 1862, Johnston, who had received reinforcements and been joined by General P. G. T. Beauregard, surprised Grant there, but in the two-day battle that followed (Shiloh) failed to defeat him. Johnston himself was among the many killed in what was, up to this point, the bloodiest battle in American history.

Grant was severely criticized in the North for having been taken by surprise. Yet with other Union victories and Farragut's capture of New Orleans, the North had taken all of the Mississippi River except for a 110-mile stretch between the Confederate fortresses of Vicksburg, Mississippi, and Port Hudson, Louisiana.

5.3 THE SUCCESS OF NORTHERN DIPLOMACY

Many southerners believed Britain and France would rejoice in seeing a divided and weakened America. The two countries would likewise be driven by the need of their factories for cotton and thus intervene on the Confederacy's behalf. So strongly was this view held that during the early days of the war, when the Union blockade was still too weak to be very effective, the Confederate government itself prohibited the export of cotton in order to hasten British and French intervention. This view proved mistaken for several reasons:

1) Britain already had on hand large stocks of cotton from the bumper crops of the years immediately prior to the war.

2) During the war the British were successful in finding alternative sources of cotton, importing the fiber from India and Egypt.

3) British leaders may also have weighed their country's need to import wheat from the northern United States against its desire for cotton from the southern states.

4) British public opinion opposed slavery.

5) Skillful northern diplomacy had a great impact. In this, Lincoln had the extremely able assistance of Secretary of State William Seward, who took a hard line in warning Europeans not to interfere, and of Ambassador to Great Britain Charles Francis Adams.

Britain therefore remained neutral and other European countries, France in particular, followed its lead.

One incident nevertheless came close to fulfilling southern hopes for British intervention. In November 1861 Captain Charles Wilkes of the U.S.S. *San Jacinto* stopped the British mail and passenger ship *Trent* and forcibly removed Confederate emissaries James M. Mason and John Slidell. News of Wilkes' action brought great rejoicing in the North but outrage in Great Britain, where it was viewed as a violation of Britain's rights on the high seas. Lincoln and Seward, faced with British threats of war at a time the North could ill afford it, wisely chose to release the envoys and smooth things over with Britain.

The Confederacy was able to obtain some loans and to purchase small amounts of arms, ammunition, and even commerce-raiding ships such as the highly successful C.S.S. *Alabama*. However, Union naval superiority kept such supplies to a minimum.

5.4   THE WAR AT SEA

The Confederacy's major bid to challenge the Union's naval superiority was based on the employment of a technological innovation, the ironclad ship. The first and most successful of the Confederate ironclads was the C.S.S. *Virginia*. Built on the hull of the abandoned Union frigate *Merrimac*, the *Virginia* was protected from cannon fire by iron plates bolted over her sloping wooden sides. In May 1862 she destroyed two wooden warships of the Union naval force at Hampton Roads, Virginia, and was seriously threatening to destroy the rest of the squadron before being met and fought to a standstill by the Union ironclad U.S.S. *Monitor*.

5.5   THE HOME FRONT

The war on the home front dealt with the problems of maintaining public morale, supplying the armies of the field, and resolving constitutional questions regarding authority and the ability of the respective governments to deal with crises.

For the general purpose of maintaining public morale but also as items many Republicans had advocated even before the war, Congress in 1862 passed two highly important acts dealing with domestic affairs in the North:

1) The Homestead Act granted 160 acres of government land free of charge to any person who would farm it for at least five years. Much of the West was eventually settled under the provisions of this act.

2) The Morrill Land Grant Act offered large amounts of the Federal government's land to states that would establish "agricultural and mechanical" colleges. Many of the nation's large state universities were founded in later years under the provisions of this act.

Keeping the people relatively satisfied was made more difficult by the necessity, apparent by 1863, of imposing conscription in order to obtain adequate manpower for the huge armies that would be needed to crush the South. Especially hated by many working class northerners was the provision of the conscription act that allowed a drafted individual to avoid service by hiring a substitute or paying $300. Resistance to the draft led to riots in New York City in which hundreds were killed.

The Confederacy, with its much smaller manpower pool on which to draw, had instituted conscription in 1862. Here, too, it did not always meet with cooperation. Some southern governors objected to it on doctrinaire states' rights grounds, doing all they could to obstruct its operation. A provision of the southern conscription act allowing one man to stay home as overseer for every twenty slaves led the non-slaveholding whites who made up most of the southern population to grumble that it was a "rich man's war and a poor man's fight." Draft-dodging and desertion became epidemic in the South by the latter part of the war.

Scarcity of food and other consumer goods in the South as well as high prices led to further desertion as soldiers left the ranks to care for their starving families. Discontent also manifested itself in the form of a "bread riot" in Richmond.

Supplying the war placed an enormous strain on both societies, but one the North was better able to bear.

To finance the northern side of the war, high tariffs and an income tax (the nation's first) were resorted to, yet even more money was needed. The Treasury Department, under Secretary of the Treasury Salmon P. Chase, issued "greenbacks," an unbacked fiat currency that nevertheless fared better than the southern paper money because of greater confidence in northern victory. To facilitate the financing of the war through credit expansion, the National Banking Act was passed in 1863.

The South, with its scant financial resources, found it all but impossible to cope with the expense of war. Excise and income taxes were levied and some small loans were obtained in Europe, yet the southern Congress still felt compelled to issue paper money in such quantities that it became virtually worthless. That, and the scarcity of almost everything created by the war and its disruption of the economy, led to skyrocketing prices.

The Confederate government responded to the inflation it created by imposing taxes-in-kind and *impressment*, the seizing of produce, livestock, etc., by Confederate agents in return for payment according to an artificially set schedule of prices. Since payment was in worthless inflated currency, this amounted to confiscation and soon resulted in goods of all sorts becoming even scarcer than otherwise when a Confederate impressment agent was known to be in the neighborhood.

Questions of constitutional authority to deal with crises plagued both presidents.

To deal with the emergency of secession, Lincoln stretched the presidential powers to the limit, or perhaps beyond the limit, of the Constitution. To quell the threat of secession in Maryland, Lincoln suspended the writ of habeas corpus and imprisoned numerous suspected secessionists without charges or trial, ignoring the insistence of pro-southern Chief Justice Roger B. Taney in *ex Parte Merryman* (1861) that such action was unconstitutional.

"Copperheads," northerners such as Clement L. Vallandigham of Ohio who opposed the war, denounced Lincoln as a tyrant and would-be dictator but remained a minority. Though occasionally subject to arrest and/or deportation for their activities, they were generally allowed a considerable degree of latitude.

Davis encountered obstructionism from various state governors, the Confederate Congress, and even his own vice president, who denounced him as a tyrant for assuming too much power and failing to respect states' rights. Hampered by such attitudes, the Confederate government proved less effective than it might have been.

5.6   THE EMANCIPATION PROCLAMATION

By mid-1862, Lincoln, under pressure from radical elements of his own party and hoping to create a favorable impression on foreign public opinion, determined to issue the Emancipation Proclamation, declaring free all slaves in areas still in rebellion as of January 1, 1863. In order that this not appear an act of panic and desperation in view of the string of defeats the North had recently suffered on the battlefields of Virginia, Lincoln, at Seward's recommendation, waited to announce the proclamation until the North should win some sort of victory. This was provided by the Battle of Antietam, September 17, 1863.

Though the Radical Republicans, pre-war abolitionists for the most part, had for some time been urging Lincoln to take such a step, northern public opinion as a whole was less enthusiastic, as the Republicans suffered major losses in the November 1862 Congressional elections.

5.7   THE TURNING POINT IN THE EAST

After his victory of the Second Battle of Bull Run, Lee moved north and crossed into Maryland, where he hoped to win a decisive victory that would force the North to recognize southern independence.

He was confronted by the Army of the Potomac, once again under the command of General George B. McClellan. Through a stroke of good fortune early in the campaign, detailed plans for Lee's entire audacious operation fell into McClellan's hands, but the northern general, by extreme caution and slowness, threw away this incomparable chance to annihilate Lee and win — or at least shorten — the war.

The armies finally met along Antietam Creek, just east of the town of Sharpsburg in western Maryland. In a bloody but inconclusive day-long battle, known as Antietam in the North but as Sharpsburg in the South, McClellan's timidity led him to miss another excellent chance to destroy Lee's cornered and badly outnumbered army. After the battle Lee retreated to Virginia, and Lincoln, besides issuing the Emancipation Proclamation, removed McClellan from command.

To replace him, Lincoln chose General Ambrose E. Burnside, who promptly demonstrated his unfitness for command by blundering into a lopsided defeat at Fredericksburg, Virginia, December 13, 1862.

MAJOR MILITARY OPERATIONS, 1863

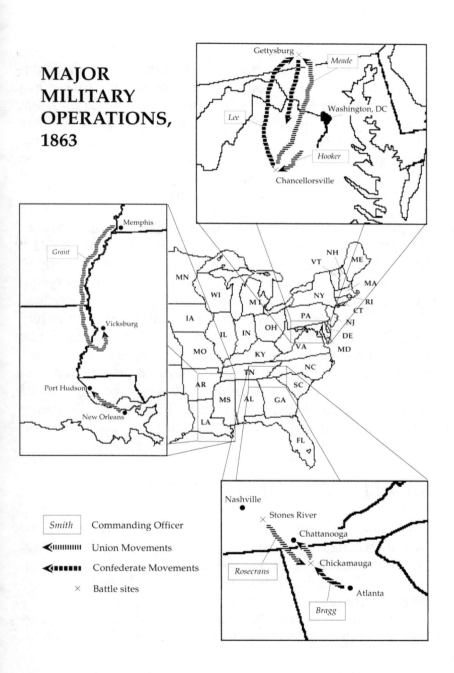

Gettysburg

Meade

Washington, DC

Lee

Hooker

Chancellorsville

Memphis

Grant

Vicksburg

Port Hudson

New Orleans

MN

WI

IA

IL

MI

IN

OH

MO

KY

AR

TN

MS

AL

GA

LA

FL

NH

VT

ME

NY

MA

RI

CT

PA

NJ

DE

VA

MD

NC

SC

Nashville

Stones River

Chattanooga

Chickamauga

Rosecrans

Bragg

Atlanta

| Smith | Commanding Officer |
| Union Movements |
| Confederate Movements |
| × | Battle sites |

Lincoln then replaced Burnside with General Joseph "Fighting Joe" Hooker. Handsome and hard-drinking, Hooker had bragged of what he would do to "Bobby Lee" when he got at him; but when he took his army south, "Fighting Joe" quickly lost his nerve. He was outgeneraled and soundly beaten at the Battle of Chancellorsville, May 5-6, 1863. At this battle the brilliant southern general "Stonewall" Jackson was accidentally shot by his own men and died several days later.

Lee, anxious to shift the scene of the fighting out of his beloved Virginia, sought and received permission from President Davis to invade Pennsylvania. He was pursued by the Army of the Potomac, now under the command of General George G. Meade, whom Lincoln had selected to replace the discredited Hooker. They met at Gettysburg; and in a three-day battle (July 1-3, 1863) that was the bloodiest of the entire war, Lee, who sorely missed the services of Jackson and whose cavalry leader, the normally reliable J. E. B. Stuart, failed to provide him with timely reconnaissance, was defeated. However, he was allowed by the victorious Meade to retreat to Virginia with his army intact if battered, much to Lincoln's disgust. Still, Lee would never again have the strength to mount such an invasion.

5.8   LINCOLN FINDS GRANT

Meanwhile Grant undertook to take Vicksburg, one of the two last Confederate bastions on the Mississippi River. In a brilliant campaign he bottled up the Confederate forces of General John C. Pemberton inside the city and placed them under siege. After six weeks of siege, the defenders surrendered, July 4, 1863. Five days later Port Hudson surrendered as well, giving the Union complete control of the Mississippi.

After Union forces under General William Rosecrans suf-

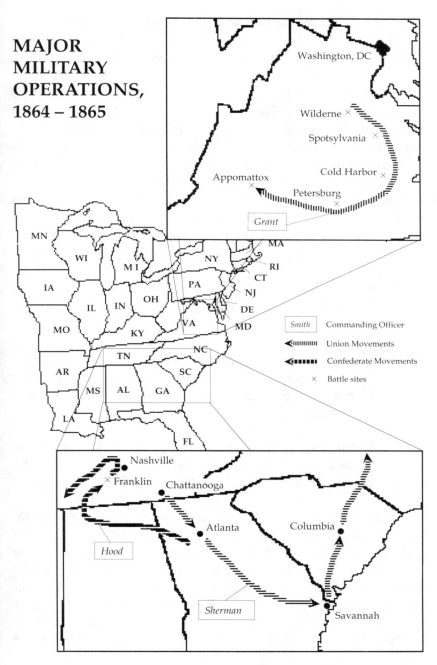

MAJOR
MILITARY
OPERATIONS,
1864 – 1865

Washington, DC

Wilderne ×

Spotsylvania ×

Cold Harbor ×

Appomattox ×

Petersburg ×

Grant

MN

WI

MI

NY

MA

RI

CT

IA

PA

NJ

IL

IN

OH

DE

MO

VA

MD

KY

Smith Commanding Officer

◄▦▦▦ Union Movements

◄▥▥▥ Confederate Movements

× Battle sites

TN

NC

AR

SC

MS

AL

GA

LA

FL

Nashville

× Franklin

Chattanooga

Atlanta

Columbia

Hood

Sherman

Savannah

63

fered an embarrassing defeat at the Battle of Chickamauga in northwestern Georgia, September 19-20, 1863, Lincoln named Grant overall commander of Union forces in the West.

Grant went to Chattanooga, Tennessee, where Confederate forces under General Braxton Bragg were virtually besieging Rosecrans, and immediately took control of the situation. Gathering Union forces from other portions of the western theater and combining them with reinforcements from the East, Grant won a resounding victory at the Battle of Chattanooga (November 23-25, 1863), in which Federal forces stormed seemingly impregnable Confederate positions on Lookout Mountain and Missionary Ridge. This victory put Union forces in position for a drive into Georgia, which began the following spring.

Early in 1864 Lincoln made Grant commander of all Union armies. Grant devised a coordinated plan for constant pressure on the Confederacy:

1) General William T. Sherman would lead a drive toward Atlanta, Georgia, with the goal of destroying the Confederate army under General Joseph E. Johnston (who had replaced Bragg).

2) Grant himself would accompany Meade and the Army of the Potomac in advancing toward Richmond with the goal of destroying Lee's Confederate army.

In a series of bloody battles (the Wilderness, Spotsylvania, Cold Harbor) in May and June of 1864, Grant drove Lee to the outskirts of Richmond. Still unable to take the city or get Lee at a disadvantage, Grant circled around to try to take both by way of the back door, attacking Petersburg, Virginia, an important railroad junction just south of Richmond and the key to that city's — and Lee's — supply lines. Once again turned back by entrenched Confederate troops Grant settled down to besiege

Petersburg and Richmond in a stalemate that lasted some nine months.

Sherman had been advancing simultaneously in Georgia. He maneuvered Johnston back to the outskirts of Atlanta with relatively little fighting. At that point Confederate President Davis lost patience with Johnston and replaced him with the aggressive General John B. Hood. Hood and Sherman fought three fierce but inconclusive battles around Atlanta in late July, then settled down to a siege of their own during the month of August.

5.9   THE ELECTION OF 1864 AND NORTHERN VICTORY

In the North discontentment grew with the long casualty lists and seeming lack of results. Yet the South could stand the grinding war even less. By late 1864 Jefferson Davis had reached the point of calling for the use of blacks in the Confederate armies, though the war ended before black troops could see action for the Confederacy. The South's best hope was that northern war-weariness would bring the defeat of Lincoln and the victory of a peace candidate in the election of 1864.

Lincoln ran on the ticket of the National Union party, essentially the Republican party with loyal or "War" Democrats. His vice-presidential candidate was Andrew Johnson, a loyal Democrat from Tennessee.

The Democratic party's presidential candidate was General George B. McClellan, who, with some misgivings, ran on a platform labeling the war a failure and calling for a negotiated peace settlement even if that meant southern independence.

The outlook was bleak for a time, and even Lincoln himself believed that he would be defeated. Then in September 1864 word came that Sherman had taken Atlanta. The capture of this vital southern rail and manufacturing center brought an enormous boost to northern morale. Along with other northern victories that summer and fall, it insured a resounding election victory for Lincoln and the continuation of the war to complete victory for the North.

To speed that victory Sherman marched through Georgia from Atlanta to the sea, arriving at Savannah in December 1864 and turning north into the Carolinas, leaving behind a 60-mile-wide swath of destruction. His goal was to impress on southerners that continuation of the war could only mean ruin for all of them. He and Grant planned that his army should press on through the Carolinas and into Virginia to join Grant in finishing off Lee.

Before Sherman's troops could arrive, Lee abandoned Richmond (April 3, 1865) and attempted to escape with what was left of his army. Pursued by Grant, he was cornered and forced to surrender at Appomattox, Virginia, April 9, 1865. Other Confederate armies still holding out in various parts of the South surrendered over the next few weeks.

Lincoln did not live to receive news of the final surrenders. On April 14, 1865, he was shot in the back of the head while watching a play in Ford's Theater in Washington. His assassin, pro-southern actor John Wilkes Booth, injured his ankle in making his escape. Hunted down by Union cavalry several days later, he died of a gunshot wound, apparently self-inflicted. Several other individuals were tried, convicted, and hanged by a military tribunal for participating with Booth in a conspiracy to assassinate not only Lincoln, but also Vice-President Johnson and Secretary of State Seward.

CHAPTER 6

THE ORDEAL OF RECONSTRUCTION

6.1 LINCOLN'S PLAN OF RECONSTRUCTION

Reconstruction began well before fighting of the Civil War came to an end. It brought a time of difficult adjustments in the South.

Among those who faced such adjustments were the recently freed slaves, who flocked into Union lines or followed advancing Union armies or whose plantations were part of the growing area of the South that came under Union military control. Some slaves had left their plantations, and thus their only means of livelihood, in order to obtain freedom within Union lines. Many felt they had to leave their plantations in order to be truly free, and some sought to find relatives separated during the days of slavery. Some former slaves also seemed to misunderstand the meaning of freedom, thinking they need never work again.

To ease the adjustment for these recently freed slaves, Congress in 1865 created the Freedman's Bureau, to provide food, clothing, and education, and generally look after the interests of former slaves.

Even before the need to deal with this problem had forced itself on the northern government's awareness, steps had been taken to deal with another major adjustment of Reconstruction, the restoration of loyal governments to the seceded states. By 1863 substantial portions of several southern states had come under northern military control, and Lincoln had set forth a policy for re-establishing governments in those states.

Lincoln's policy, known as the Ten Percent Plan, stipulated that southerners, except for high-ranking rebel officials, could take an oath promising future loyalty to the Union and acceptance of the end of slavery. When the number of those who had taken this oath within any one state reached ten percent of the number who had been registered to vote in that state in 1860, a loyal state government could be formed. Only those who had taken the oath could vote or participate in the new government.

Tennessee, Arkansas, and Louisiana met the requirements and formed loyal governments but were refused recognition by Congress, which was dominated by Radical Republicans.

The Radical Republicans, such as Thaddeus Stevens of Pennsylvania, believed Lincoln's plan did not adequately punish the South, restructure southern society, and boost the political prospects of the Republican party. The loyal southern states were denied representation in Congress and electoral votes in the election of 1864.

Instead the Radicals in Congress drew up the Wade-Davis Bill. Under its stringent terms a majority of the number who had been alive and registered to vote in 1860 would have to swear an "ironclad" oath stating that they were now loyal and had *never been* disloyal. This was obviously impossible in any former Confederate state unless blacks were given the vote, something Radical Republicans desired but southerners definitely did not. Unless the requisite number swore the "ironclad" oath, Congress would not allow the state to have a government.

Lincoln killed the Wade-Davis bill with a "pocket veto," and the Radicals were furious. When Lincoln was assassinated the Radicals rejoiced, believing Vice President Andrew Johnson would be less generous to the South or at least easier to control.

6.2   JOHNSON'S ATTEMPT AT RECONSTRUCTION

To the dismay of the Radicals, Johnson followed Lincoln's policies very closely, making them only slightly more stringent by requiring ratification of the Thirteenth Amendment (officially abolishing slavery), repudiation of Confederate debts, and renunciation of secession. He also recommended the vote be given to blacks.

Southern states proved reluctant to accept these conditions, some declining to repudiate Confederate debts or ratify the Thirteenth Amendment (it nevertheless received the ratification of the necessary number of states and was declared part of the Constitution in December 1865). No southern state extended the vote to blacks (at this time no northern state did, either). Instead the southern states promulgated Black Codes, imposing various restrictions on the freedom of the former slaves.

6.3 FOREIGN POLICY UNDER JOHNSON

On coming into office Johnson had inherited a foreign policy problem involving Mexico and France.

The French Emperor, Napoleon III, had made Mexico the target of one of his many grandiose foreign adventures. In 1862, while the U.S. was occupied with the Civil War and therefore unable to prevent this violation of the Monroe Doctrine, Napoleon III had Archduke Maximilian of Austria installed as a puppet emperor of Mexico, supported by French troops. The U.S. had protested but for the time could do nothing.

With the war over, Johnson and Secretary of State Seward were able to take more vigorous steps. General Philip Sheridan was sent to the Rio Grande with a military force. At the same time Mexican revolutionary leader Benito Juarez was given the tacit recognition of the U.S. government. Johnson and Seward continued to invoke the Monroe Doctrine and to place quiet pressure on Napoleon III to withdraw his troops. In May 1866, facing difficulties of his own in Europe, the French emperor did so, leaving the unfortunate Maximilian to face a Mexican firing squad.

Johnson's and Seward's course of action in preventing the extension of the French Empire into the western hemisphere strengthened America's commitment to and the rest of the world's respect for the Monroe Doctrine.

In 1866 the Russian minister approached Seward with an offer to sell Alaska to the U.S. The Russians desired to sell Alaska because its fur resources had been largely exhausted and because they feared that in a possible war with Great Britain (something that seemed likely at the time) they would lose Alaska anyway.

Seward, who was an ardent expansionist, pushed hard for the purchase of Alaska, known as "Seward's Folly" by its critics, and it was largely through his efforts that it was pushed through Congress. It was urged that purchasing Alaska would reward the Russians for their friendly stance toward the U.S. government during the Civil War at a time when Britain and France had seemed to favor the Confederacy.

In 1867 the sale went through and Alaska was purchased for $7,200,000.

6.4 CONGRESSIONAL RECONSTRUCTION

Southern intransigence in the face of Johnson's relatively mild plan of Reconstruction manifested in the refusal of some states to repudiate the Confederate debt and ratify the 13th amendment. The refusal to give the vote to blacks, the passage of black codes, and the election of many former high-ranking Confederates to Congress and other top positions in the southern states, played into the hands of the Radicals, who were anxious to impose harsh rule on the South. They could now assert that the South was refusing to accept the verdict of the war.

Once again Congress excluded the representatives of the southern states. Determined to reconstruct the South as it saw fit, Congress passed a Civil Rights Act and extended the authority of the Freedman's Bureau, giving it both quasi-judicial and quasi-executive powers.

Johnson vetoed both bills, claiming they were unconstitutional; but Congress overrode the vetoes. Fearing that the Supreme Court would agree with Johnson and overturn the laws, Congress approved and sent on to the states for ratification (June 1866) the Fourteenth Amendment, making constitutional the laws Congress had just passed. The Fourteenth Amendment stipulated the following:

1) defined citizenship and forbade states to deny various rights to citizens,

2) reduced the representation in Congress of states that did not allow blacks to vote,

3) forbade the paying of the Confederate debt, and

4) made former Confederates ineligible to hold public office.

With only one southern state, Tennessee, ratifying, the amendment failed to receive the necessary approval of three fourths of the states. But the Radicals in Congress were not finished. Strengthened by victory in the 1866 elections, they passed, over Johnson's veto, the Military Reconstruction Act, dividing the South into five military districts to be ruled by military governors with almost dictatorial powers. Tennessee, having ratified the Fourteenth Amendment, was spared the wrath of the Radicals. The rest of the southern states were ordered to produce constitutions giving the vote to blacks and to ratify the Fourteenth Amendment before they could be "readmitted." In this manner the Fourteenth Amendment was ratified.

Realizing the unprecedented nature of these actions, Congress moved to prevent any check or balance from the other two branches of government. Steps were taken toward limiting the jurisdiction of the Supreme Court so that it could not review cases pertaining to congressional Reconstruction policies.

This proved unnecessary as the Court, now headed by Chief Justice Salmon P. Chase in place of the deceased Taney, readily acquiesced and declined to overturn the Reconstruction acts.

To control the President, Congress passed the Army Act, reducing the President's control over the army. In obtaining the cooperation of the army the Radicals had the aid of General Grant, who already had his eye on the 1868 Republican presidential nomination. Congress also passed the Tenure of Office Act, forbidding Johnson to dismiss cabinet members without the Senate's permission. In passing the latter act, Congress was especially thinking of Radical Secretary of War Edwin M. Stanton, a Lincoln holdover whom Johnson desired to dismiss.

Johnson obeyed the letter but not the spirit of the Reconstruction acts, and Congress, angry at his refusal to cooperate, sought in vain for grounds to impeach him until in August 1867, Johnson violated the Tenure of Office Act (by dismissing Stanton) in order to test its constitutionality. The matter was not tested in the courts, however, but in Congress, where Johnson was impeached by the House of Representatives and came within one vote of being removed by the Senate. For the remaining months of his term he offered little further resistance to the Radicals.

6.5 THE ELECTION OF 1868 AND THE 15TH AMENDMENT

In 1868 the Republican convention, dominated by the Radicals, drew up a platform endorsing Radical Reconstruction. For president, the Republicans nominated Ulysses S. Grant, who had no political record and whose views — if any — on national issues were unknown. The Vice Presidential nominee was Schuyler Colfax.

Though the Democratic nomination was sought by Andrew Johnson, the party knew he could not win and instead nominated former Governor Horatio Seymour of New York for president and Francis P. Blair, Jr. of Missouri for vice president. Both had been Union generals during the war. The Democratic platform mildly criticized the excesses of Radical Reconstruction and called for continued payment of the war debt in greenbacks, although Seymour himself was a hard-money man.

Grant, despite his enormous popularity as a war hero, won by only a narrow margin, drawing only 300,000 more popular votes than Seymour. Some 700,000 blacks had voted in the southern states under the auspices of army occupation, and since all of these had almost certainly voted for Grant, it was clear that he had not received a majority of the white vote.

The narrow victory of even such a strong candidate as Grant prompted Republican leaders to decide that it would be politically expedient to give the vote to all blacks, North as well as South. For this purpose the 15th amendment was drawn up and submitted to the states. Ironically, the idea was so unpopular in the North that it won the necessary three-fourths approval only with its ratification by southern states required to do so by Congress.

6.6 POST-WAR LIFE IN THE SOUTH

Reconstruction was a difficult time in the South. During the war approximately one in ten southern men had been killed. Many more were maimed for life. Those who returned from the war found destruction and poverty. Property of the Confederate government was confiscated by the Federal government, and dishonest Treasury agents confiscated private property as well. Capital invested in slaves or in Confederate war bonds was lost. Property values fell to one-tenth of their pre-war level. The economic results of the war stayed with the South for decades.

The political results were less long-lived but more immediately disturbing to southerners. Southerners complained of widespread corruption in governments sustained by federal troops and composed of "carpetbaggers," "scalawags" (respectively the southern names for northerners who came to the South to participate in Reconstruction governments and southerners who supported the Reconstruction regimes), and recently freed blacks.

Under the Reconstruction governments, social programs were greatly expanded, leading to higher taxes and growing state debts. Some of the financial problems were due to corruption, a problem in both North and South in this era when political machines, such as William Marcy "Boss" Tweed's Tammany Hall machine in New York, dominated many northern city governments and grew rich.

Southern whites sometimes responded to Reconstruction governments with violence, carried out by groups such as the Ku Klux Klan, aimed at intimidating blacks and white Republicans out of voting. The activities of these organizations were sometimes a response to those of the Union League, an organization used by southern Republicans to control the black vote. The goal of southerners not allied with the Reconstruction governments, whether members of the Ku Klux Klan or not, was "redemption" (i.e., the end of the Reconstruction governments).

By 1876 southern whites had been successful, by legal means or otherwise, in "redeeming" all but three southern states. The following year the Federal government ended its policy of Reconstruction and the troops were withdrawn, leading to a return to power of white southerners in the remaining states.

Reconstruction ended primarily because the North lost interest. Corruption in government, economic hard times brought on by the Panic of 1873, and general weariness on the part of northern voters with the effort to remake southern society all sapped the will to continue. Diehard Radicals such as Thaddeus Stevens and Charles Sumner were dead.

6.7 CORRUPTION UNDER GRANT

Having arrived in the presidency with no firm political positions, Grant found that the only principle he had to guide his actions was his instinctive loyalty to his old friends and the politicians who had propelled him into office. This principle did not serve him well as President. Though personally of unquestioned integrity, he naively placed his faith in a number of thoroughly dishonest men. His administration was racked by one scandalous revelation of government corruption after another. Not every scandal involved members of the executive branch, but together they tended to taint the entire period of Grant's administration as one of unparalleled corruption.

6.7.1 *The "Black Friday" Scandal*

In the "Black Friday" scandal, two unscrupulous businessmen, Jim Fiske and Jay Gould, schemed to corner the gold market. To further their designs, they got Grant's brother-in-law to convince the President that stopping government gold sales would be good for farmers. Grant naively complied, and many businessmen were ruined as the price of gold was bid up furiously on "Black Friday." By the time Grant realized what was happening, much damage had already been done.

6.7.2 *The Credit Mobilier Scandal*

In the Credit Mobilier scandal, officials of the Union Pacific Railroad used a dummy construction company called Credit

Mobilier to skim off millions of dollars of the subsidies the government was paying the Union Pacific for building a transcontinental railroad. To ensure that Congress would take a benevolent attitude toward all this, the officials bribed many of its members lavishly. Though much of this took place before Grant came into office, its revelation in an 1872 congressional investigation created a general scandal.

6.7.3 The "Salary Grab Act"

In the "Salary Grab Act" of 1873, Congress voted a 100% pay raise for the President and a 50% increase for itself and made both retroactive two years back. Public outrage led to a Democratic victory in the next congressional election and the law was repealed.

6.7.4 The Sanborn Contract Fraud

In the Sanborn Contract fraud, a politician named Sanborn was given a contract to collect $427,000 in unpaid taxes for a 50% commission. The commission found its way into Republican campaign funds.

6.7.5 The Whiskey Ring Fraud

In the Whiskey Ring fraud, distillers and treasury officials conspired to defraud the government of large amounts of money from the excise tax on whiskey. Grant's personal secretary was in on the plot, and Grant himself naively accepted gifts of a questionable nature. When the matter came under investigation, Grant endeavored to shield his secretary.

6.7.6 The Bribing of Belknap

Grant's secretary of war, W. W. Belknap, accepted bribes from corrupt agents involved in his department's administration of Indian affairs. When the matter came out, he resigned to escape impeachment.

Discontentment within Republican ranks with regard to some of the earlier scandals as well as with the Radicals' vindictive Reconstruction policies led a faction of the party to separate and constitute itself as the Liberal Republicans. Besides opposing corruption and favoring sectional harmony, the Liberal Republicans favored hard money and a laissez-faire approach to economic issues. For the election of 1872 they nominated New York *Tribune* editor Horace Greeley for president. Eccentric, controversial, and ineffective as a campaigner, Greeley proved a poor choice. Though nominated by the Democrats as well as the Liberal Republicans, he was easily defeated by Grant, who was again the nominee of the Radicals.

6.8   ECONOMIC ISSUES UNDER GRANT

Many of the economic difficulties the country faced during Grant's administration were caused by the necessary readjustments from a wartime back to a peacetime economy.

The central economic question was deflation versus inflation or, more specifically, whether to retire the unbacked paper money, greenbacks, printed to meet the wartime emergency, or to print more.

Economic conservatives, creditors, and business interests usually favored retirement of the greenbacks and an early return to the gold standard.

Debtors, who had looked forward to paying off their obligations in depreciated paper money worth less than the gold-backed money they had borrowed, favored a continuation of currency inflation through the use of more greenbacks. The deflation that would come through the retirement of existing greenbacks would make debts contracted during or immediately after the war much harder to pay.

Generally, Grant's policy was to let the greenbacks float until they were on par with gold and could then be retired without economic dislocation.

Early in Grant's second term the country was hit by an economic depression known as the Panic of 1873. Brought on by the overexpansive tendencies of railroad builders and businessmen during the immediate post-war boom, the Panic was triggered by economic downturns in Europe and, more immediately, by the failure of Jay Cooke and Company, a major American financial firm.

The financial hardship brought on by the Panic led to renewed clamor for the printing of more greenbacks. In 1874 Congress authorized a small new issue of greenbacks, but it was vetoed by Grant. Pro-inflation forces were further enraged when Congress in 1873 demonetized silver, going to a straight gold standard. Silver was becoming more plentiful due to western mining and was seen by some as a potential source of inflation. Pro-inflation forces referred to the demonetization of silver as the "Crime of '73."

In 1875 Congress took a further step toward retirement of the greenbacks and return to a working gold standard when, under the leadership of John Sherman, it passed the Specie Resumption Act, calling for the resumption of specie payments (i.e., the redeemability of the nation's paper money in gold) by January 1, 1879.

Disgruntled proponents of inflation formed the Greenback party and nominated Peter Cooper for president in 1876. However, they gained only an insignificant number of votes.

6.9   THE COMPROMISE OF 1877

In the election of 1876, the Democrats campaigned against corruption and nominated New York Governor Samuel J. Tilden, who had broken the Tweed political machine of New York City.

The Republicans passed over Grant, who was interested in another term and had the backing of the remaining hard-core Radicals, and turned instead to Governor Rutherford B. Hayes of Ohio. Like Tilden, Hayes was decent, honest, in favor of hard money and civil service reform, and opposed to government regulation of the economy. In their campaigning, the Republicans resorted to a tactic known as "waving the bloody shirt." Successfully used in the last two presidential elections, this meant basically playing on wartime animosities, urging northerners to vote the way they had shot, and suggested that a Democratic victory and a Confederate victory would be about the same thing.

This time the tactic was less successful. Tilden won the popular vote and led in the electoral vote 184 to 165. However, 185 electoral votes were needed for election, and 20 votes, from the three southern states still occupied by Federal troops and run by Republican governments, were disputed.

Though there had been extensive fraud on both sides, Tilden undoubtedly deserved at least the one vote he needed to win. Congress created a special commission to decide the matter. It was to be composed of five members each from the Senate, the House, and the Supreme Court. Of these, seven were to be Republicans, seven Democrats, and one an independent. The

Republicans arranged, however, for the independent justice's state legislature to elect him to the Senate. When the justice resigned to take his Senate seat, it left all the remaining Supreme Court justices Republican. One of them was chosen, and in a series of eight-to-seven votes along straight party lines, the commission voted to give all 20 disputed votes — and the election — to Hayes.

When outraged congressional Democrats threatened to reject these obviously fraudulent results, a compromise was worked out. In the Compromise of 1877, Hayes promised to show consideration for southern interests, end Reconstruction, and withdraw the remaining Federal troops from the South in exchange for Democratic acquiescence in his election.

Reconstruction would probably have ended anyway, since the North had already lost interest in it.

"The ESSENTIALS" of HISTORY

REA's **Essentials of History** series offers a new approach to the study of history that is different from what has been available previously. Compared with conventional history outlines, the **Essentials of History** offer far more detail, with fuller explanations and interpretations of historical events and developments. Compared with voluminous historical tomes and textbooks, the **Essentials of History** offer a far more concise, less ponderous overview of each of the periods they cover.

The **Essentials of History** provide quick access to needed information, and will serve as a handy reference source at all times. The **Essentials of History** are prepared with REA's customary concern for high professional quality and student needs.

UNITED STATES HISTORY

1500 to 1789 From Colony to Republic
1789 to 1841 The Developing Nation
1841 to 1877 Westward Expansion & the Civil War
1877 to 1912 Industrialism, Foreign Expansion & the Progressive Era
1912 to 1941 World War I, the Depression & the New Deal
1941 to 1988 America as a World Power

EUROPEAN HISTORY

1450 to 1648 The Renaissance, Reformation & Wars of Religion
1648 to 1789 Bourbon, Baroque & the Enlightenment
1789 to 1848 Revolution & the New European Order
1848 to 1914 Realism & Materialism
1914 to 1935 World War I & Europe in Crisis
1935 to 1988 World War II & the Iron Curtain

WORLD HISTORY

Ancient History (4,500BC to 500AD)
The Emergence of Western Civilization
Medieval History (500 to 1450AD)
The Middle Ages

If you would like more information about any of these books,
complete the coupon below and return it to us or go to your local bookstore.

RESEARCH & EDUCATION ASSOCIATION
61 Ethel Road W. • Piscataway, New Jersey 08854
Phone: (908) 819-8880

Please send me more information about your History Essentials Books

Name _____

Address _____

City _____ State _____ Zip _____

"The ESSENTIALS" of Math & Science

Each book in the ESSENTIALS series offers all essential information of the fi[eld]
it covers. It summarizes what every textbook in the particular field must include, a[nd]
is designed to help students in preparing for exams and doing homework. T[he]
ESSENTIALS are excellent supplements to any class text.

The ESSENTIALS are complete, concise, with quick access to needed inform[a-]
tion, and provide a handy reference source at all times. The ESSENTIALS [are]
prepared with REA's customary concern for high professional quality and stud[ent]
needs.

Available in the following titles:

Advanced Calculus I & II
Algebra & Trigonometry I & II
Anthropology
Automatic Control Systems /
   Robotics I & II
Biology I & II
Boolean Algebra
Calculus I, II & III
Chemistry
Complex Variables I & II
Differential Equations I & II
Electric Circuits I & II
Electromagnetics I & II
Electronic Communications I & II

Electronics I & II
Finite & Discrete Math
Fluid Mechanics /
   Dynamics I & II
Fourier Analysis
Geology
Geometry I & II
Group Theory I & II
Heat Transfer I & II
LaPlace Transforms
Linear Algebra
Mechanics I, II & III
Modern Algebra

Numerical Analysis I & II
Organic Chemistry I & II
Physical Chemistry I & II
Physics I & II
Real Variables
Set Theory
Statistics I & II
Strength of Materials &
   Mechanics of Solids I &[II]
Thermodynamics I & II
Topology
Transport Phenomena I &[II]
Vector Analysis

*If you would like more information about any of these books,
complete the coupon below and return it to us or go to your local bookstore.*

REA's **Test Preps**
The Best in Test Preparation

The REA "Test Preps" are far more comprehensive than any other test series. They contain more tests with much more extensive explanations than others on the market. Each book provides several complete practice exams, based on the most recent tests given in the particular field. Every type of question likely to be given on the exams is included. Each individual test is followed by a complete answer key. **The answers are accompanied by full and detailed explanations.** By studying each test and the pertinent explanations, students will become well-prepared for the actual exam.

REA has published 20 Test Preparation volumes in several series. They include:

Advanced Placement Exams
Biology
Calculus AB & Calculus BC
Chemistry
English Literature & Composition
European History
United States History

College Board Achievement Tests
American History
Biology
Chemistry
English Composition
French
German
Spanish
Literature
Mathematics Level I & II

Graduate Record Exams
Biology
Chemistry
Computer Science
Economics
Engineering
General
Literature in English
Mathematics
Physics
Psychology

FE - Fundamentals of Engineering Exam
GMAT - Graduate Management Admission Te
MCAT - Medical College Admission Test
NTE - National Teachers Exam
SAT - Scholastic Aptitude Test
LSAT - Law School Admission Test
TOEFL - Test of English as a Foreign Langua

RESEARCH & EDUCATION ASSOCIATION
61 Ethel Road W. • Piscataway, New Jersey 08854
Phone: (908) 819-8880

Please send me more information about your Test Prep Books

Name _____

Address _____

City _____ State _____ Zip _____